LESSONS FROM THE SPEECHLESS

HOW TO RUN A SUCCESSFUL BUSINESS

First published in the UK in 2022 by Pentre Publications

Pentre House, Leighton Welshpool Powys SY21 8HL

ISBN 978-095205407-8

Cover design: Carol Harris
Book design: Paul Harris

WHAT READERS HAVE SAID

Carol Harris has created a book for entrepreneurs who know they need to up their game to grow. Imagine looking around your place, and the scissors, the mirror, the stamps, the opera glasses etc. are now all programmed (by you) so you remember the keys to improving your performance. I recommend reading a couple of these enticing tidbits per day, taking a minute to embed them into your experience, and then notice how your productivity and delight increase.
Shelle Rose Charvet
Author of the international bestseller Words That Change Minds

This latest book by Carol Harris provides a particularly useful resource to those running or about to set up a business organisation. Drawing on a wide range of sources as well as everyday items to illustrate the advice being provided, it combines wisdom and practical experience in an interesting and amusing way. More specifically, this book offers valuable insights and practical guidance based on the writer's wide experience as a management researcher, business owner, board director, publisher, editor and author.
Dr Bernard Barry
Director of Yarra International, a Melbourne-based management consultancy. Dr Barry previously held professorial appointments at Cranfield, Melbourne and Monash universities and has been a visiting professor at the universities of Auckland and Lyon.

It is so easy to get bogged down in all the complexities of running a business, until you can't see the wood from the trees! *Lessons from the Speechless* brings a fresh perspective on well known business principles in a novel format, sprinkled with tongue in cheek humour and historical facts.
Sian Roberts
Director and co-founder of The Game Change Project CIC

Carol's compact stories bring the world of inanimate objects to life, revealing time-old wisdom in the most unexpected of places. Thought-provoking, fun and energising! A unique and eclectic blend of innovative ideas, infused with a light-hearted soul that will inspire you and will never age.
Fleur Sclarandis
Trainer and facilitator

Are you starting a business, but confused about how to make it successful? Carol's book has vital advice. It is easy to understand and gives you direction on how to manage, and build, a business. Topics include the importance of focus – if we do not focus, we will not build momentum. Also consistency, which is essential for business success. And productivity, because if we are not productive it affects the bottom line in business. This book is well worth reading and Carol is an excellent mentor and business coach.
Rosemary O'Shaughnessy
Podcaster, trainer and digital content manager

I have always admired Carol's 'out of the box' approach. I have read many business books in my time and this one provides easy reading on what can be a dry topic. It is short and to the point; no waffle, just good advice. The light-hearted explanation of the opportunities and pitfalls of running a business is clear, concise, easy to follow and humorous. This book could help direct you when starting a business, giving a much better chance of success. I commend the book to you and hope you enjoy and learn from what is a great read.
Robert Robinson
MBE, FRICS, FSLCC

Carol has created a refreshing way of looking things we often take for granted but are nearly always important. It's easy to miss their importance. The style is light-hearted, and therefore memorable, as well as thought provoking. The latter is extremely valuable - it helps to dispel complacency and the carelessness that can often go with it. There is some good learning here
Doug Strycharczyk
Author. CEO, AQR International

Interesting common sense business book for young entrepreneurs, unravelling the mysteries of running a business. Each section is a common-sense business lesson with useful tips for easily adopting good habits for running a business. Each one also has an interesting and relevant 'factoid' about the inanimate and speechless things we share our households with. Can be picked up and read at any time and in any order – no need to feel guilty about not reading the book in one go.
Jeff Herman
FCA, MBA, FIC; Managing Director Blue-Plate Consulting Ltd.

An interesting approach designed for people considering starting a new business and with reminders of what it takes for us all.
Barry Tuckwood
MBA CEng, MICE, MIStructE, CMC MIC. Independent consultant in Strategy, Change and Project Management, and academic working with international students through their MBAs.

Reading the stories is a fun reminder of the best practices in business without being lectured at. Rather clever really. And it makes a good coffee table read – or for some light relief in the bathroom)!
David Rigby
MD of SmartCoachingTraining.com Focusing on diversity, psychological safety, wellness, profiling and development via coaching, training, consulting, keynote speaking and writing

CONTENTS

INTRODUCTION

If you are new to running a business, or perhaps would like to brush up on some skills, this book is a light-hearted explanation of some of the key areas involved.

Quite a few of the little scenarios that follow were originally posts on LinkedIn – they weren't intended to be a book but, as people were asking if they would be, I decided to put them together in one place.

There are plenty of books about business out there already – including a few of mine. I didn't think the world needed another general business book, but thought maybe a few tips on what's important might spark some interest.

If that's the case with you, then you can easily find out more online, attend a course, do some reading or talk to other people to develop your effectiveness.

There are four sections to this book:

- **What about me?** Personal improvement
- **How do you do?** Relationship skills
- **Where do I start?** Business processes
- **What's in it for them?** Community and beyond

I hope the pages that follow amuse you, add to your knowledge and generate some curiosity about how business works. And if you're just contemplating a career as a business owner, perhaps my book will show you that it doesn't always have to be serious. I find humour is, in itself, an important attribute in business – it doesn't do to take everything (including oneself) too seriously.

WHAT ABOUT ME?
Personal improvement

When starting a business, it's important to pay attention to yourself. It will be *your* business and will reflect *your* abilities, interests and performance. So it's vital to be as effective as you can.

This first section is all about personal improvement.

SELF AWARENESS

Do you think your self-awareness is good, or do people sometimes misinterpret the signals you give? Monitoring yourself is an important skill, as this little object observes!

MIRROR ON THE WALL

"Hello decorative mirror".

"Hello – good to see you again".

"Yes, good to see me again".

"Hmmmmm"!

"What's new with you today"?

"Not a lot, just hanging here as usual, but nobody's stopped by so far".

"Well it's been quiet today, no visitors".

"Or maybe they're just being more observant and don't need me"'.

"What do you mean"?

"Well, some people don't seem to be very self-aware. The only times they notice themselves are when they look in a mirror. Incidentally, did you know that mirrors have been around for about 8,000 years. The earliest ones were pieces of polished stone. Later, bronze, iron and steel mirrors appeared, then metal-coated glass mirrors about 2,000 years ago. Then the first modern silvered glass mirrors were produced in 1835. But I digress".

"So, what's your point about being more observant then"?

"The point is that sometimes you need to notice yourself, so you have an idea about how you're coming across to other people".

"And why is that important"?

"Because if you aren't aware of how you look and sound, and what you're doing, you might give a wrong impression or, worse, upset or annoy people unintentionally".

"You mean it's OK to upset and annoy people if you mean to do it"?

"Now then, don't make fun of me; you know perfectly well what I mean".

"Yes, sorry, of course I do. But if people don't always notice themselves, is there anything they can do to improve their self-awareness"?

"Yes, a simple thing is for them to do a running commentary in their head (not out loud or people may get the wrong impression)! So they might, for example, say (in their head) 'I'm putting on my left shoe', or 'I'm picking up the kettle', or 'I'm smiling', or 'I'm taking deep breaths', or 'I feel warm', or 'I'm imagining how this afternoon's meeting will go', or 'I'm looking directly at the camera',

or 'I'm telling myself I must do some exercise this morning'. That way they'll get into the habit of self-observation, which is an important skill".

"Gosh, you know a lot, mirror".

"Comes from all that observing I do myself – it's my only function, so I've got really good at it. Just hope a few more people learn to do the same".

How about considering your facial expressions, your voice tonality, the distance you stand from people, your mannerisms, your gestures, what you say and what your posture's like? There are many things you can notice about yourself, and self-awareness is a skill that's well worth developing.

BEING CHEERFUL

Are you usually optimistic? Or do you have 'down days'? Do you allow external factors to influence your mood? If you run a business, it helps to look on the bright side. Here are some ideas that might be useful.

SUNFLOWER ON THE WORKTOP

"Hello sunflower – welcome to our house. I'm pleased to have you here, especially as you've such a long history – I've been told that sunflowers were grown by indigenous people in America about five thousand years ago".

"Yes, I believe that's true and thanks so much for inviting me; it's lovely to be here. Much nicer than being blown about in the field – it was beginning to get quite cold there in the last few days".

"Yes, here too, which is why we've just put some heating on and brought a few of our plants in from their summer holidays on the patio".

"I saw a few of them through the window; seemed quite chilly. I think they were a bit envious of me being here in your kitchen. But then it's always good to look on the bright side".

"Difficult for you to do anything else – you only have bright sides; bright petals, bright pollen, shiny leaves – quite the little ray of sunshine".

"Well sunshine comes from within too, you know. I was told that when I was a tiny seed on one of my mum's flowers. "Be cheerful", she said "and life will be more fun".

"I must tell that to some of my business colleagues, sunflower. A few of them could do with cheering up. They often get disheartened about things and listen to others who are negative or miserable and seem to want everyone else to feel the same way".

"That's no good. Nothing nice can come from negative thinking. Of course everything in the garden isn't always rosy (or sunny, in my case), but finding something you can do to make things seem better is good for you. When we had people walking around our fields, before you picked me, I heard some of them saying that if you control your thoughts then you can have nicer feelings. Apparently it all feeds back to useful hormones circulating in your body and creating better health for you in the long run".

"How did you remember all that? You don't have a notepad to record it all".

"Of course flowers don't have notepads; what a ridiculous thought. But some of us do have good memories. I heard of some mimosa plants which were in an experiment. Those plants curl up their leaves if they're disturbed, so some of them were dropped 60 times onto something soft to see if they could use their memory to change their behaviour. And eventually they stopped closing their leaves when they were dropped, because they knew they weren't going to get harmed after all".

"That's probably because they were exhausted, not because they were learning".

"Exactly what I thought, but no, when they were then put in a shaker, they closed up again, so they weren't too exhausted to respond to a different potential threat. And then when they were dropped again they remembered that hadn't harmed them previously, so they stopped closing up again. Their memory was still there after 28 days. Even bees forget things in a couple of days, so almost a month for a plant to remember is excellent. That's why it's not surprising I remembered those conversations about positive thoughts".

"How remarkable. And what can people do to have more positive thoughts, sunflower"?

"They can visualise good outcomes; they can say nice things to themselves in a pleasant tone of voice; they can recall good experiences – there are lots of things they can do to give themselves a positive experience rather than a miserable one".

"Well that's good to know. And I hope you have a positive experience in our kitchen".

"It's been fine so far, but maybe a little more water, a bit of plant food and some more conversation would make me feel even better. And possibly a couple more flowers to keep me company"?

"Don't push your luck".

What do you do if you want to cheer yourself up? And what else can you think of, which might make you feel more cheerful?

FOCUS

Are you easily able to pay attention to important things?

OPERA GLASSES ON THE TABLE

"Hello little opera glasses; good to see you again".

"It's been a very long time. I've felt quite neglected. By the way, you know some people call me binoculars – and there are different kinds of

those, all originating from the invention of the telescope in the 17th century. But I'm actually opera glasses and very much prettier than ordinary binoculars, so I'm glad you appreciate me – even though you don't take me out much".

"Sorry. It's ages since I went to a live opera, so I haven't needed you, but if I do, you'll be the first to know"

"An outing would be good – I'd enjoy that. It would be great to have something to look at apart from this room. Although I do see one interesting thing through my clear container".

"What do you mean"?

"I see you pottering about when you think nobody's looking. Instead of getting on with your work you're sorting clothes, or taking photos through the window. How do you think you'll get ahead with that kind of attitude?

"There's nothing wrong with taking a break, you know".

"Very true, but there's a big difference between a rest and a lack of focus".

"Lack of focus"?

"Of course. When people look through me, they see clearly. All they focus on is the specific thing that's important to them at the time. If they kept swivelling me around, they'd just get a blur".

"So you're saying I should only have a narrow field of vision"?

"No, that's not right either. It's about deciding what's important and then having a really sharp focus on it for the duration. Set boundaries and time limits and don't get diverted while you're on that project. Then you can relax afterwards and potter to your heart's content".

"I do really focus on things I'm interested in; I don't have a problem with that. But, in common with lots of other business owners, I find it harder to maintain focus when I'm doing things that don't really excite me".

"Yes, you're not alone in that, but it's important to work at it if you want to be successful".

"Maybe I should keep you with me, instead of in your container – you're specifically made for seeing things clearly and it would remind me to do the same".

"Great – how about starting now".

Are there things you keep putting off? May be time to review what you work on.

CONSISTENCY

How consistently do you take action in your business? Is what you do erratic? Do you do things when you feel like it, or do you do them regardless of your energy levels or motivation? Maybe take a tip from my toothbrushes!

TOOTHBRUSHES IN THE BATHROOM

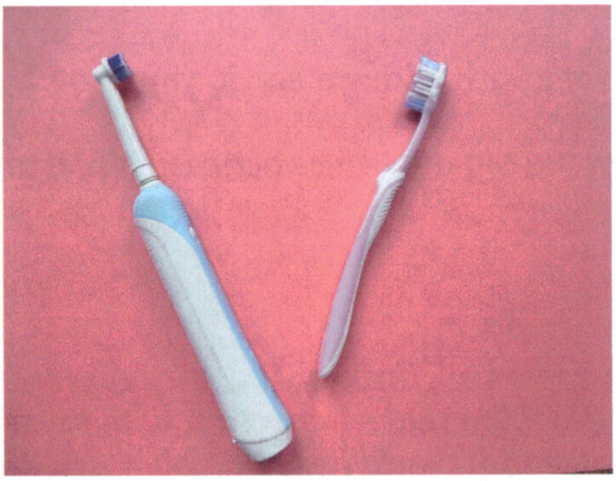

"Hello toothbrushes. Doesn't seem any time at all since I saw you last".

"That's because it isn't! You use us each day without fail. Something people have done for a very long time. Did you know that people used to have twigs to clean their teeth and 'chew sticks' were used in ancient Babylon over 5,000 years ago. And then the first bristle toothbrushes were invented by the Chinese over 1,000 years ago, made from the very stiff hairs of pigs that lived in that harsh climate".

"No. I didn't know that. But I do know you're really important. An awful thing I read in a magazine a few months ago was that quite a few people forget to brush their teeth. Isn't that weird – how can you forget something like that"?

"Doesn't surprise us any more than knowing how a lot of people who run a business aren't consistent in their activities. It's not good enough to do things occasionally. Having a regular pattern to what you do makes a difference, whether that's brushing your teeth or growing your income".

"Why do you think a regular pattern is important, toothbrushes"?

"Well one thing that makes effective business owners stand out is that they're consistent in what they do. They decide what level of activity is needed in order to get the results they want and then they make sure they do that activity. They don't let anything stand in their way".

"But surely they must have off-days; times when they really don't feel like doing anything".

"Yes, of course they do; they're only human after all – unlike us. It's no skin off our noses if we work all day every day (or it wouldn't be if we had noses, that is). But humans aren't like us and they let themselves get distracted easily, or allow themselves to lose energy and motivation".

"And is that lack of dedication inevitable".

"No, it isn't. Just look at elite sportspeople. They train consistently, whether they feel like it or not. Of course sometimes they overdo it and have to be careful to avoid exhaustion and injury, but usually they have a carefully mapped out schedule and they stick to it until they've achieved their goal. Successful business owners do the same".

"So it's simple really – make a plan and follow it. Do what you need to do. Make sure you don't overdo things and keep going, consistently, until you get the results you want".

"You've got it. Now, let's get on with cleaning your teeth".
How dedicated are you to being consistent?

BEING FLEXIBLE

Do you like consistency and structure in your business activities? Do you enjoy the predictability of a routine? Or are you more able to 'go with the flow' and vary what you do if needed? Maybe this will throw some light on the subject.

PAPER CLIPS ON THE DESK

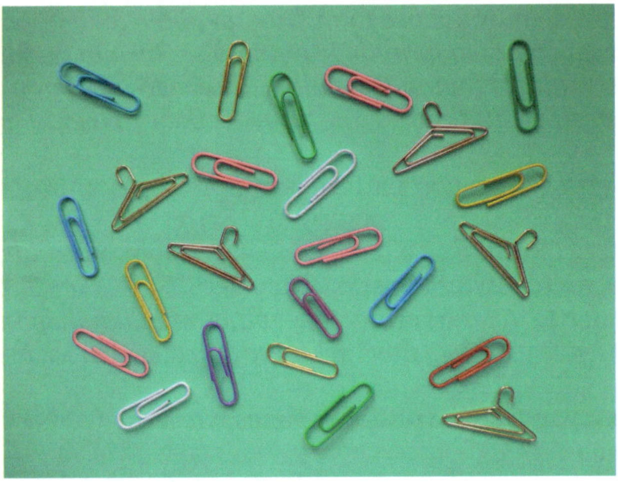

"Hello paper clips – you're such a lovely collection of colours".

"Thank you. We often compare notes about whose colour is best, but actually we think we're all pretty good".

"It seems a shame to keep you in a drawer actually – I'd almost rather have you on display somewhere".

"Well there's nothing to stop you doing that – and we'd enjoy being out in the light".

"OK, you can come out then – let's find you somewhere more interesting to live".

"That would be good; nobody's suggested that to us before. By the way, did you notice that some of us are different".

"Oh yes, a few of you are shaped like coat hangers – how strange".

"It's so you can hang us up after you've clipped papers into us; isn't that a great idea. Of course, we weren't always made of metal or plastic you know. In the thirteenth century, papers started to be fastened together with ribbons through their corners. Later, those ribbons were waxed to make them stronger and easier to do up and undo. And all that continued for six hundred years, until paperclips like us were invented".

"Well that's good to know. And you're certainly useful".

"And flexible too. How many of your business colleagues could say that about themselves, we wonder. Flexibility's really important in business you know".

"So I believe. What flexibility lessons could we humans learn from you, paperclips"?

"Well we have to be able to clip together small numbers of sheets of paper, and also larger numbers. If there are more sheets, we have to change our approach to accommodate them all – and humans also need to change approach if circumstances change".

"I see. And anything else"?

"Yes. If we do have to divert from our normal pattern – or shape, should we say, we have the flexibility to go back to it when the unusual situation passes – so it's about being flexible just for as long as needed. Oh, and also business trainers have used us as subjects for creative thinking - you must have heard of the exercise about 'How many uses can you think of for a paperclip".

"Yes, yes, I have. But I'd only thought about it in terms of creativity, not flexibility. But of course it's that too – if you think outside the box, you can adapt to lots of different situations as needed. And that's a good life lesson, as well as a business one".

"Certainly is. Now where are you going to put us so we can be seen. We quite fancy the wall behind your desk. That way all your video-conferencing colleagues can see us too and be reminded about being flexible themselves.

"Good idea paperclips – let's do it now".

How important is flexibility in your own business?

PACING YOURSELF

Have you ever suffered from 'burn-out'? Do you 'burn the candle at both ends'? Have you pushed yourself beyond what's sensible just to get a task done"? Well, if so, you're not alone. It's so easy to get sucked in to overload and it's counter-productive. See if these innocuous objects can throw light on how we live our lives and run our businesses.

SANDALS ON THE FLOOR

"Hello sandals – good to see you".

"Well we were pleased NOT to see YOU yesterday".

"Charming! How rude are you two"?

"We're not rude at all; just pleased you didn't wear us".

"So why was that"?

"Because if you wear shoes, or other clothes, non-stop they wear out faster; thought you'd have known that".

"Well, I did, but I didn't really think it mattered".

"Yes it does. It's like you working non-stop without breaks. In the end your body gives up from exhaustion. Giving yourself time to rest and recover is important, even if it's just twenty minutes every hour or so to change the scenery, look out of a window, go for a short walk, alter your eye focus, drink some water or close your eyes and relax. Then you'll feel better and be more productive".

"That sounds great, but I often forget to do it".

"You just need to notice the signals your body gives you".

"Oh, what are they"?

"Things like feeling tired, yawning, losing concentration, wanting to go to the loo, needing a drink, getting dry eyes, fidgeting – lots of things can be a sign that your body (and your mind) needs a break".

"Well how did you sandals become so clever"?

"We don't just sit here, you know. Our hearing is superb so we listen to all those TED talks and news items you nod off to and we're really well informed. Unlike you".

"I heard that! But thanks for the tip and I'll remember to give you and my other clothes a rest too, so you have a longer and better life as well. Thanks sandals".

"You're welcome. It's just one thing we've learned over our really long history. You know, the oldest known footwear were sandals made of sagebrush bark. They were discovered in caves in Oregon and are at least 10,000 years old. So we've had a long time to get to know humans and be able to help them".

How do you keep yourself on top of things?

STAYING COOL – MAINTAINING EMOTIONAL CONTROL

Do you have a calm disposition, or do you easily get het up? Are you able to 'keep your cool' whatever happens? Another object gives an opinion.

SPARKLY FAN ON THE TABLE

"Hello sparkly fan. I haven't given you an outing for a long time".

"No, I used to be taken to all kinds of places, but that seems a lifetime ago".

"Such a shame. And a bigger shame that the times have passed when fans like you were seen everywhere. In some circles, an outfit wouldn't have been acceptable without a fan".

"A long-gone world. We're pretty much museum pieces now, apart from very hot countries, of course, where we're still a necessity, although I did hear a rumour that we're set for a comeback as the climate becomes hotter. Did you know that we fans have been around for at least 5,000 years"?

"As long as that? It's quite a history".

"And there weren't any folding fans until relatively recently - and even then we were mainly used by royalty and regarded as status symbols. People who weren't so well off still used fans with fixed feathers".

"So a fan like you would have been quite special all along – I bet you have some interesting stories to tell".

"Well they're mostly about being cool".

"What, having designer labels and trendy footwear, you mean"?

"No, of course not – think sensibly! That meaning of cool is quite new, and I don't like it one bit; no self-respecting fan would. What I mean is staying emotionally cool, rather than getting heated. What your business associates should aim for".

"How should they aim to stay cool"?

"By being in control of their emotions. Not getting frustrated or angry at people or circumstances, but maintaining their equilibrium".

"That's a big word for a little fan! But surely you need energy and dynamism in order to get things done and be successful".

"Of course you do. I'm not suggesting people submerge all their responses to things – just use their energy in productive ways. Maybe you should print that advice on to a new fan. Lots of fans used to have words printed on them, you know. There have been advertising fans, biblical fans and no end of humorous fans – like the one printed with 'How to play Whist and not lose your temper', which is a bit like the topic we've been discussing".

"So it is. Leave it with me and I'll see what I can do".

"And see what you can do about another outing for me too please, while you're about it".

Does anything make you lose your cool?

MAINTAINING A BALANCE

Is work the main focus of your life, or do you have plenty of other things that you spend time on?

SCALES ON THE SHELF

“Hello scales. You’ve got a good view from up there, haven’t you”.

“Yes, we have. We see everyone coming and going and know what they’re up to”.

“If you weren’t so large, you’d be down here with the other scales, but they’re very small and don’t need weights, so we tend to use them most of the time”.

“It’s a shame, really, because we scales have a great history and it’s a pity we’re not more appreciated. Did you know the oldest weighing scales were found near present day Pakistan and are about four thousand years old. They just had two plates at the ends of a beam fixed on an upright pole, so that the object to be measured could be put on one plate and then compared to some stone cubes on the other plate until a balance was reached”.

"And in ancient Egypt there were murals showing the God Anubis weighing the hearts of people who had died, in order to decide which ones were worthy of entering heaven".

"Goodness, that's a bit different from what we do in our kitchen – quite glad our uses are more down to earth nowadays".

"Yes, but there are lots of other aspects to balance apart from weighing objects. How about considering balance in your life"?

"Why do you say that, scales"?

"Because when we listen to some people who visit you, they don't seem to have much of a balance in what they do. Some only talk about work, some only talk about their ailments, some only talk about their children. They don't seem to realise that just focusing on one thing isn't healthy – particularly if it's work".

"I do agree. Not only is it unhealthy to have little time for recreation, exercise, learning and so on, but it's very tedious for other people if you only have one topic of conversation".

"Unless theirs is the same, of course – although not everyone enjoys hearing about other people's activities, even if they are similar to their own".

"So what do you suggest people do to have more of a balanced life"?

"A good thing would be to spend a week or so monitoring their time. They could make a chart with each day split into separate hours, so they can write down the main activity they've engaged in during each hour. Then, if there isn't much variation in their activities, they could think of some things they really enjoy, or things they want to do, but haven't made time for in the past, and then substitute those for an hour or so a week. And then – over several weeks - they could gradually increase that time spent on other things".

"So they end up with more variety and, hopefully, more interests. Sounds good to me".

Do you maintain a balance in your own life? If not, the little chart exercise mentioned above is well worth doing.

DECISION MAKING

Do you find it easy to make decisions, or do you sometimes dither? Take a look at this.

SNOOKER BALLS ON THE TABLE

"Hello coloured balls – you all seem to be a bit huddled together".

"That's because nobody's done much with us today".

"What were you expecting them to do"?

"Well usually they arrange us nicely and then take turns to poke us into the little pockets around the table with those long wooden things".

"Cues".

"No, only two people usually".

"Pardon"

"We thought you mentioned queues".

"No – that's silly. I mean the wooden things are called cues".
"Yes, of course. You know people have played ball games for hundreds of years. It started with lawn games, a bit like croquet, and then moved indoors to wooden tables which had green cloths so they looked like

grass. This became so popular that Shakespeare even mentioned it in his play Antony and Cleopatra. And it wasn't silly to mention queues, because the cue sticks were originally called queues, derived from a French word for tail, but that eventually changed to cues as you spell it now. Before that, balls were hit with sticks called maces, but they had large heads and were difficult to use and, for a long time, only men were allowed to use cues and women had to use a mace in case they tore the cloth with the sharper cue"!

"So no anti-discrimination laws in those days then".

"No. And did you know that originally snooker balls were made of wood but, because they warped easily, they started being made of ivory, until elephants had almost been hunted to extinction. Luckily artificial balls were then created, but they had a problem; if you hit those balls too hard they could explode"!

"That wouldn't make for a very safe game".

"No, it wouldn't. Anyway, now we have different coloured balls and each colour has a different value. You humans try to score more points than your opponents when you play with us. But some of you do better than others, of course".

"Well, some people are just better players".

"Maybe, but a lot of it comes down to making good decisions about how to hit us balls. It's the same with businesses, of course, some people are better at creating successful businesses because they make good decisions".

"Isn't that just a matter of luck"?

"Not at all. There are lots of things you can do to improve your decision-making".

"Such as what"?

"You can make sure you're clear on your goals and do research to collect information. You can test different options before deciding what to do (that works well in advertising, for example, where you can check out the effectiveness of different wording before spending a lot of money on adverts). You can consider the consequences of a particular decision –

including the pros and cons of taking a particular step or not taking it – and remember to think about the impact on other people of any decision you make; also think about the impact of making a wrong decision and ask yourself if a particular decision fits with who you are and what your values are. Some people make snap decisions, while others need to mull things over, or get lots of positive evidence before deciding anything. And many decisions are made based on emotion, but then justified with reason".

"That's a lot to think about".

"Certainly is. Glad we're just coloured balls and the only decision we have to make is whether to chat to you or just sit here minding our own business".

"In that case, I'll make the decision for you; I'm off to get a glass of water, so you can have some peace and quiet for the rest of the afternoon".

Do you have a process for making decisions?

PRIORITISING

Do you ever find yourself wondering what's the most important thing you need to do? If so, this may help.

COLANDER ON THE WALL

"Hello colander, you look bright today".

"Yes, I'm enjoying the sunshine and just being able to lounge about".

"I'd like to do that myself, but I'm far too busy to even sit down".

"Well my advice is - keep hold of the important things and let all the lesser ones just drain away. We colanders have been doing that for such a long time – you know we've been used for over three thousand years".

"Easier said than done, colander. All you have to do is sit there while someone else decides what you'll keep and what you can let go of. In fact they don't even have to decide - it's automatic with you; the unimportant stuff just goes away of its own accord".

"Well there's nothing stopping you doing that too. If you make a list of the most important things you have to do then, automatically - just like with me - the other, less important, things drop off the bottom. And, just as I have a sink to catch the unwanted stuff, you can have a file of the things you've let go of and you can come back to them any time you like - if you really want to, that is".

"Sounds easy".

"Yes, it is. Just get that list done and you'll be able to sit in the sun as well. Have a great weekend".

So how about doing one of those lists for yourself.

TIME MANAGEMENT

Do you struggle with time? Can you fit everything into 24 hours, or are there things that haven't been done at the end of most days? If so, maybe this will help.

SEE-THROUGH CLOCK ON THE SHELF

"Hello see-through clock. I'm always intrigued by being able to see how you work".

"I'm intrigued by being able to see how you work too (or rather how you don't work)"?

"What's that supposed to mean"?

"Well you're always finding time to do things you want to do, while saying you don't have enough time for the things you need to do".

"How true; you're very perceptive, clock".

"So if you know it's true, how come you don't do anything about it"?

"Life's too short to spend it all working, or cleaning, or doing boring stuff".

"Yes, but if you want to pay the bills, then you need to pay attention to time. Would you like some tips on that".

"Like isn't the right word, but if you mean would I benefit from knowing how to get on with those things I don't enjoy, then that would certainly be useful. Go ahead".

"Well here are three things I think you'd find helpful. The first is to take neglected tasks as signals. So if something's been sitting on your desk for a week and you haven't dealt with it, then it's a motivation issue that needs addressing, not a time management one. Decide if you absolutely have to do it yourself and, if so, find a way of making it more tolerable. One way is to work on it for only five minutes at a time and then spend five minutes doing something that's more fun; that should make it easier".

"Sounds good, I'll give that a go. I have to do some accounts later today, so I'll intersperse that with sorting some old photos and enjoying the memories they bring back. What's your second tip"?

"Do things at your best time of day. You know about clocks, because you have me sitting in your kitchen and you wear a watch and you see the news with Big Ben chiming at the start. But did you know living things have body clocks too – inbuilt ways of noticing time passing, and resting or sleeping when appropriate. Your body clock is personal to you, and you'll have times during the day when you find it easier to do physical activities and times when you find it easier to do mental activities. If you pay attention to this you can allocate tasks to your 'best times' which will make them seem easier to get done".

"Yes, I knew about that but don't always bear it in mind when I'm working, so that's a good reminder. And what's your third tip"?

"Well in some countries, people make a habit of stopping eating before they're completely full up. It's healthier than stuffing your face until you're absolutely bloated. The same applies to managing your time. Stop before you're exhausted; that way you don't use up all your energy – whether it's mental or physical – and then you can go on to the next thing with some reserves in place".

"Those are really useful things, clock. And maybe I'll even wind you up now – it'll make a change from you winding me up"!

What's your favourite strategy for doing those less than fascinating tasks?

IMPRESSION MANAGEMENT

Have you ever wondered what people think of you? If so, this might be of interest.

PIG ON THE LANDING

"Hello pig - you're looking very cheerful".

"Of course I am; I really enjoy life. However we pigs are very misunderstood animals".

"Yes, I know that. I've always loved pigs since I was a child. My family used to go to Weymouth on our annual holiday and we passed a piggery just outside the town. Of course I had to get out and admire the inhabitants".

"Of course you did - nothing better looking than a pig – especially a Raku one. Did you know Raku is a special type of pottery, which originated over 500 years ago, where clay objects are removed from the kiln when it's at its hottest temperature. This results in the items cooling extremely quickly, giving each piece a unique colour and pattern"?

"Well, I didn't know about that, but I can see why you'd say pigs are good looking. I used to keep rare-breed pigs which looked great (how I acquired them is an amusing story, which features in my book Some Stories of my Life and there are lots of photos of them in another of my books called A Guide to Traditional Pig Keeping)".

"That's quite enough about you, let's get back to pigs. As I said, pigs are often misunderstood; many people believe us to be unintelligent, dirty and bald. But in fact we're highly intelligent, incredibly clean (an hour-old piglet will make its way from under a heat lamp to the other side of a shed in order to have a wee - it wouldn't dream of soiling its bed like a horse or cow would) and we are quite hairy. I remember one of your own Kune Kune pigs had hair well over a foot long. So there's a few myths dispelled for your readers".

"Thank you pig. So what does any of this have to do with business"?

"Well business owners should consider how they, and their businesses, are perceived by others? Do people know 'the real you'? Do you have a personal or business brand which effectively represents your activities? And do you ever create the 'wrong' impression - either unintentionally or (worse) unknowingly? If so, you could learn a lesson from pigs. Once people properly get to know a pig they understand our characters, abilities and qualities. And you can make sure people understand you by monitoring the impressions you create, considering other people's possible perceptions before speaking or acting, and doing some research into your branding to make sure it truly represents what you offer. And if you employ other people, or work with associates, then do make sure the impression they create fits with you and your business too. Managing perceptions is an important part of business life, so give it the attention it deserves".

"That's quite a lot of insights from a pig. I knew you were bright, but didn't realise you had a business mind too".

"Absolutely - never underestimate a pig".

Impression management is an area of study that's well worth looking into.

GETTING TASK SIZES RIGHT

Do you sometimes bite off more than you can chew – or get submerged by the 'small stuff'. Perhaps this will help.

EGG SLICER IN THE KITCHEN DRAWER

"Hello egg slicer – you seem a bit cramped in the drawer today".

"Well you put all those other gadgets on top of me – what do you expect? Don't suppose you'd like to be squashed under a garlic press and a jar opener".

"No, don't expect I would, but then I'm not made of metal as you are".

"Just because I'm metal doesn't mean I'm uncrushable. You know we egg slicers have very thin wires, which can be misused, or used differently. Some of us, for example, can be played as string instruments".

"Don't be silly. Who on earth would use an egg slicer to play music"?

"Well there's a recording of one English experimental music group which did a concert in Hackney and, during it, John Balance played an egg slicer solo and called it a 'mini-harp' ".

"How extraordinary. Whatever next. Anyway, do come out for a bit of exercise. I have four eggs I'd like you to help with".

"Only four – hardly worth getting out of bed (sorry drawer) for".

"Well that's all I need today, but you're so good at it. You've been with me such a long time, and you've already been mended once, but I've never found another slicer as good as you".

"Flatterer! I suppose you'd also like me to give you some business advice while I'm cutting up your eggs".

"That would be great – what's your latest insight"?

"Well many people don't seem to be able to differentiate between tasks, and get submerged by irrelevant things. They could take a lesson from me. First I slice the eggs lengthways – that makes pretty big chunks, but then I slice them across, which makes smaller chunks, and finally I slice them across again, in a different direction, which makes tiny chunks. You can do the same with work tasks. Go through them and pick out the biggest projects, then the medium sized ones and then the tiny ones. Then, each day, unless there are any exceptionally urgent ones you have to do immediately, you can decide whether to focus on one big one, a couple of medium ones, or lots of tiny ones; you can't do them all, so having an idea of how much time and energy each one will take can help you plan".

"I like that. Thanks egg slicer – sometimes things are easier than you think. Now let's get you washed and back home until next time".
How about considering the size of tasks you set yourself.

CARRY ON LEARNING

Does your business take up all your time? Are you so busy with day to day activities that you don't spend any time on learning new things? Here's one little bird who knows all about that....

PENGUIN ON THE FILING CABINET

"Hello penguin. You're such a smart bird with your orange beak and your bright eyes".

"Yes, I am. I like to keep myself looking good; you never know when someone might spot you, so I do try to look my best. But I wish you'd turn me round a bit more. I can look out of the window, which does have a lovely view, but it means I'm not facing your computer screen, so I can't see the online events clearly, only hear what's being said".

"I didn't realise you were interested in all of that".

"Yes, of course I am. Everyone should be interested in learning new things, even if they aren't always specifically related to their business".

"Why do you think that's so important, penguin"?

"Because you can't stand still – unless you're a wooden penguin like me of course! The world's changing at an incredible rate and new things are happening all the time. If you don't carry on learning then you're likely to fall behind in your business, and competitors with more of an eye on new developments are likely to overtake you".

"Yes, that's true. I've had to learn about new aspects of social media, data storage, online marketing and video conferencing, to name just a few".

"Well it's good for you that there's so much information available now. I only have these two books and I have to just absorb as much information from them as I can – not easy when you only have the soles of your feet to do it with! But there's so much online now that there's no excuse for not having access to data and techniques on any subject under the sun. Talking of which, it's very bright in here and sometimes it's hard to see the screen because of reflections from the window. How about fixing that venetian blind that's been sickly for months now"?

"Yes, we need to do that. Been too busy watching webinars to get round to it"!

"I've noticed. Don't overdo the learning though; you should make sure you keep a balance between learning and 'real' work".

"Thanks for reminding me. And do you have any other requests while we're at it"?

"Well if you could maybe leave some wildlife videos on when you're out of the room that would be great; I might spot some fellow penguins which would be nice – and also maybe learn something new about how they spend their lives. But don't put one on about the Arctic – we don't live there, as many people think, that's for polar bears, not us".

What plans do you have to learn something new this year?

LEARN AND BENEFIT FROM FAILURE

Does the thought of 'failure' dismay you, or do you see it as an opportunity to learn?

DEAD BONSAI TREE ON THE TABLE

"Hello Bonsai tree – how's your day going"?

"Oh, you know, much the same as usual – nice to be able to look out of the window and see what's going on".

"Yes – you have great views from your table, so you're not going to be bored. What do you think about when you look out there"?

"All kinds of things. Sometimes I remember when I was alive and had all the other Bonsai trees around me – we were quite a little community. You know Bonsai trees have a long history – and we started in China, not Japan as most people believe".

"That's interesting – so how did Bonsai come about"?

"Well in China it was thought that reducing things in scale could help people gain access to their magical properties. This goes back well over 2,000 years and growing dwarf trees in containers started about 1,300 years ago. Then Japan started producing Bonsai trees in accordance with Zen Buddhism. Also, because Japan is tiny in comparison with China, the range of landscape forms there was much more limited. Oh, and the twisted forms of some of the trees were said to be similar to yoga postures, which bent back on themselves and re-circulated vital fluids; presumed to be the cause of long life".

"What a fascinating history – such a pity your own life was so short".

"And that's your fault for not looking after me properly. Although I can't complain, because your failure to keep me alive resulted in people being able to see my beautiful branches, which had been hidden by my leaves. And my branches now support the pretty little tin birds you've hung on me. So you've managed to turn the situation into something of benefit – a good lesson to learn".

"Thanks Bonsai tree – I'll look on failure differently from now on. If something doesn't work out, you should see what went wrong, so you can do better next time, and also see if you can turn the 'failed' result into something equally good, if not better. As you say, a good lesson".

Do you have any 'failures' you can learn lessons from?

FITTING ACTIVITIES TO LIFE STAGES

Career choices and activities may change throughout your life. Does what you do relate to your own stage of development?

YELLOW DATES IN THE KITCHEN

"Welcome, dates. Good to see you. It's been a long time since any of you came to our house".

"Yes, we're not seen very often in this country and there are only a few months when we're available anyway. Did you know that dates have been farmed for about nine thousand years and we can grow in clusters of up to a hundred. So we have lots of company while we're growing up".

"No, I didn't know that – how interesting. We usually only see dried dates, or sometimes bottles of date syrup, but I love you yellow dates – you're my favourite".

"Thank you so much – it's good to be appreciated. But I think you should put some of us in your fridge now, or we'll start ripening quickly".

"That's a good idea, dates. I think you're great when you're fresh and yellow and really hard, and I love dried dates too, but I'm not keen on ones that are just ripening – they go very brown and soggy and I don't like their texture at all".

"Well it's all part of our stages of development – a bit like your business colleagues".

"How are you like them"?

"Well, if they're sensible, they'll take advantage of their own stages of development and enhance them. Being dates, we can't do that, of course; we have to just accept what development is forced upon us by our age and the environment. But humans are different and they can be more selective, or choose to speed things up".

"So what do you think they should do to make the most of their lives"?

"We're no experts, just being pieces of fruit but, since you ask, we think they could copy us. We have three stages – and so do they – youth, maturity and later life. So if they're young, they can make good use of their energy and enthusiasm to learn new things, broaden their horizons and see what they're best suited to. In their middle years they could focus more on the things they've found work well for them, explore them in more depth, and perhaps become really knowledgeable and skilful at their main areas of activity. And in their later years they can perhaps develop interests that might be more 'fringe' but give them a lot of personal pleasure. There's so much to choose from and it's well worth exploring".

"Thanks dates – so you're saying people should use their preferences and personality as a base and then develop their skills so they can have a successful business and a great life. Now let's prolong your life by putting you in the fridge and letting your own personalities come to fruition (oooooh, sorry for the pun)!

Do you re-assess your choices as you go through life?

BEING ACCOUNTABLE

How do you make sure you get things done? Being accountable can help.

POSTAGE STAMP IN THE BOOK

"Hello postage stamp. Good to see you. I like stamps"

"That's interesting – we have a long history you know. In the 12th century, Henry 1 appointed messengers to carry letters for the government. Henry 111 gave them uniforms and Edward 1 instituted posting houses where they could change horses. Later 'Haste. Post haste' was written on them by hand. Henry V111 created the Royal Mail in 1516 and in those days the recipient paid for the postage, not the sender. And the first postage stamp was issued in 1840 – the Penny Black".

"Well thanks for the history lesson, but I need your help today".

"That's good. I've been sitting around in your postage book for weeks waiting to be used".

"Well I don't need stamps every day. Usually I take letters and parcels to the post office van and they sort out postage for me. But today I just want to walk down to the post box, so I need to put a stamp on myself".

"Why on earth would you need to put a stamp on yourself? You're far too big to go through the slot in the post box".

"Are you being deliberately silly? Of course I'm not going to post myself. I meant I was going to put a stamp on an envelope myself".

"Yes, I know. I was trying to be funny, but obviously it didn't work".

"Clearly not. Anyway, let's get you onto my letter now so I can catch the afternoon post".

"Before you do that, are you aware that posting a letter to yourself can be useful".

"Here we go again. Why do you keep coming up with silly things today"?

"This is NOT silly. It's a basic principle of getting things done that humans should make themselves accountable for their actions".

"I know that, but what's it got to do with posting letters to yourself – I can't see the connection".

"You don't have to go to the bother of finding someone else to be accountable to – although actually that's often the best course of action. You can also be accountable to yourself. And one way of doing that is to write down the things you want to accomplish in a letter and send it to yourself; writing on the envelope 'Open on – (and whatever date you choose)', so you have a check on whether you've done those things by the date you set".

"I suppose that makes sense, but it sounds a bit expensive to buy postage stamps every time you want to remember to do something".

"Well you could simply address an envelope to yourself and put it somewhere you'll remember to open on the date you've selected. So then when you do open the envelope you can check that you have, in fact, taken the action".

"Actually that sounds a really good idea – I like it. Have you got a friend in there with you? If so, we'll do two letters now – the one I was going to send anyway and another to me".

"And what's yours going to say"?

"Buy more postage stamps".

"An excellent choice".

Do you have an accountability system or partner? And has that worked well for you?

CHANGING YOUR BELIEFS

Do you have strong beliefs that never change? Do you sometimes get frustrated when others have beliefs you find odd or counter-productive? Here's a few thoughts on that topic...

FLYING PIGS ON THE STAIRCASE

"Hello flying pigs. You have a great view from up there; I expect you've seen lots of things over the years".

"Yes, lots. People coming and going, the view out of the window, the water that came through the ceiling before the gutters were fixed – never a dull moment. And then there are the visitors who think pigs can't fly".

"Well lots of people have limited belief systems. Nothing you can do about it".

"Not true – we think if people are helped to question their thinking, or see comparable examples with different outcomes, they might change. And it's particularly sad when people use that 'pigs might fly' expression about themselves – especially when it limits their business potential".

"How do you mean"?

*"Well we've heard some of your visitors saying things like 'Me run a business – pigs might fly', or 'I'm never going to get that idea off the ground - pigs might fly' or even 'Nobody's going to buy this product – pigs might fly'. Such a shame, because they're killing their success before it's begun. Of course, that kind of saying isn't new – the original one was **Pigs fly in the ayre with their tayles forward**, which was found in a list of proverbs in a 1616 dictionary".*

"Not heard that one but, as you say, it *is* sad that people think in that way. I've heard those kind of comments myself. So how do you think I could help people to change their beliefs"?

"Well, if they don't believe they could start a business, you might ask if they know anyone like themselves who has ever started a business – someone of their age, background, personality and so on. The chances are they could think of someone – if not a person they know personally, then maybe someone on TV for example".

"Good idea. Anything else"?

*"If they say their idea won't work, you could tell them about someone who's persevered with an idea until it **has** succeeded. And if they don't believe their product will sell, you can mention a product that wasn't instantly recognised as useful, but went on to be a great income producer".*

"And any other bright ideas"?

"Well if all else fails, you could agree with them".

"How's that going to help"?

"Sometimes, if you agree that something's a bad idea – and even exaggerate how bad it is, the person will realise they actually ***DO*** *believe in it. At that point they are quite likely to start telling you about why it* ***IS*** *good after all".*

"Sort of reverse psychology then".

"Yes, it's actually based on provocation, but you have to know what you're doing and be careful you don't undermine someone's self-esteem. Done effectively, and with the use of humour as well, it's a great approach, but is probably more for the professional to use with clients than the 'average person' to use with their friends and colleagues".

"Well that's an interesting approach. Sounds as if it needs some training though, so I'll find out more before trying that last one out. Thanks pigs – and keep hanging in there".

Have any of your beliefs ever changed and, if so, how did that come about?

CREATIVITY

Do you think everything you produce has to be novel? Here's another viewpoint.

TRILOBITE ON THE WINDOWSILL

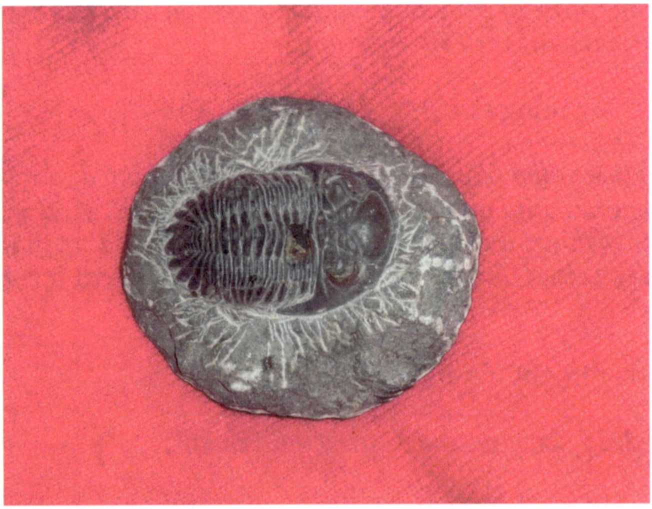

"Hello trilobite - you've been there a long time".

"Not at all – in terms of my lifespan (deathspan?) it's a nanosecond; I've been around for almost 300 million years".

"And I thought I was old! So what have you learned in all that time"?

"Re-inventing the wheel is good. Things go in cycles (sorry – almost a pun). People think they've created something unique, but often it's just a modification".

"So you're saying that innovation is often re-creation; a product doesn't have to be completely new, just a bit different".

"Exactly. And that's ecologically sound too – modify instead of create and you may also save valuable resources".

"A good lesson - thanks trilobite".

What could you modify to create a 'new' produce or service?

KEEPING UP TO DATE

Have you ever wondered how 'with it' you need to be? Do you sometimes feel defeated by the pace of change? Would you like to be as up to date as possible with as much as possible? Maybe our green friend can help.

GREEN TILE BEHIND THE BATH

"Hello green tile, you look very elegant today".

"Don't I always"?

"Yes, of course. I didn't mean to offend you. It's just that now there's a lot of sunshine about you really sparkle".

"Thanks. I like the sunshine; it does show me off to advantage".

"And your design is stunning, not like the plain tiles each side of you".

"Nice of you to say that. I'm quite pleased with myself actually, although I did wonder if anyone would still like me".

"Why's that? I can't imagine anyone not liking you".

"I think you may be biased. When I was young my colour was trendy, although that word wasn't used then, of course. And my style was bang up to date. But nowadays everyone wants plain surfaces and dull, neutral colours, so I'm very old fashioned. Not as old fashioned as some though, because tiles have been around for thousands of years – some of us possibly as much as 25,000 years, because we're basically just baked clay. And lots of us are made of Terracotta – which just means baked earth".

"Well I like you, even if you're not the newest kid on the block".

"That's a great attitude, but you won't get far in business thinking like that".

"What do you mean".

"Well things change so quickly nowadays, that if you don't keep yourself informed of the latest developments you'll lag behind, and then people won't want to use your services".

"So being up to date is always good"?

"Well not absolutely always. For example it's not ecologically sound to always have the latest bit of equipment – the newest phone, the faster printer, the bigger screen. If you do that, then you're constantly disposing of perfectly usable items and, sadly, many find their way to landfill or go up in smoke. But it can be good to have the latest bit of information in your field, the most up to date report on relevant trends and the newest app to help you monitor your health. You have to use a bit of common sense".

"I heard that common sense is an oxymoron".

"Who are you calling stupid"?

"No, I meant that common sense isn't always used. I think you're right that it's important to be up to date in your field, but that doesn't always mean buying bright, shiny objects to prove it".

"Well done; we agree. Now are you going to have that bath or not? No point in me sticking to the wall looking pretty unless I'm functional as well. Just get a move on please before you get glued to the spot too".

What do you think is important about being up to date? How do you decide how far to go in following trends or having the latest gizmo?

PERSONAL DEVELOPMENT

Do you find time to enhance your knowledge and skills, or has running your business pushed all that to the back of the queue for your time? Updating yourself is important, as some common flowers explain.

POPPIES BEHIND THE COOKER

"Hello artificial poppies, you're all so pretty with your bright colours and happy faces".

"Well our colours would be even brighter if you washed us more often, you know".

"Sadly I do know, but I forget until the cobwebs remind me".

"We don't have cobwebs; how rude".

"Sorry, no you don't, but they aren't far away".

"So how about giving us a makeover then? Everyone deserves to get refreshed from time to time – even your business colleagues. Many of them are probably as static as we are and don't update their skills or knowledge as often as they should".

"Very true, poppies. I know a lot of people who haven't done a training course, or changed their ways of working, for years".

"No excuse really. With all the webinars and videos and podcasts and blogs around nowadays everyone can learn new things at the touch of a button. And a lot of it's free too. All they need to do is allocate a bit of time to their own development and they could be far ahead of their competitors. What a shame they're stuck in their old habits".

"Well what's the best way for them to start"?

"Just pick one area – for example being organised, doing presentations, thinking positively or learning how to relax and then, when they've learned more about that, and practised effectively, they can move on to something else. Simple".

"Yes it is. And the one thing *I'm* going to focus on first is learning the best ways to keep artificial flowers looking good".

"That's an excellent skill to develop. We're looking forward to showing off our clean, shiny petals and leaves to all your visitors (if you ever have any again, that is)!

Which topics are at the top of your own list for personal development?

HAVE A MENTOR

Sometimes, having another person to act as a sounding-board, give you advice and jolly you along can be helpful. Let's see how that works...

SOCKS IN THE DRAWER

"Hello socks, you're in a bit of a huddle".

"Yes, we were just comparing notes about how frequently we'd left our drawer; it's not often we're outside together".

"Well it's difficult for me to wear more than one pair of you at a time – and in winter some of you are far too short and thin to be useful anyway".

"Well thanks for the compliment! Great to know we have only limited use".

"Yes, but you really *are* useful in the summer. And a variety of colours and patterns is great; when I can find you that is – you see to be really good at hiding".

"There's a reason for that".

"Really"?

"Yes. If you remember, some of us were once put in with other washing and our dark colours ran into the lighter clothes. That didn't make us popular".

"So what's that got to do with hiding then – I can't not use you at all; that would be pointless".

"We believe you humans have what you call mentors – other people with more experience who can give you good advice and listen to your ideas before you take action".

"Yes, that's true".

"Well, we had a mentor as well".

"I find that hard to believe".

"Well it's true. It was a much older sock – very dark purple. By the way, did you know that socks have a long history. We may have been worn in the Stone Age, because cave paintings seem to show what look like socks made out of animal skins and furs. Then the ancient Greeks made us out of matted animal hair and the Romans sewed fabric to make fitted socks. You know, Roman tablets found in the north of England included the instruction to 'send more socks'. And the first knitted socks were made in Ancient Egypt. But we digress. The old purple sock told us we should always look out through the gap at the top of our drawer and, if we saw light coloured clothes being taken to the washing machine, we should hide, so as not to get in with them and make them look horrible".

"So you've been monitoring my clothes all this time and saving me from washing disasters".

"Yes, we have. And it's all thanks to your old sock. By the way, you might give that sock an outing too some time – it's made a real contribution to your household, so a bit of daylight from time to time would be really welcome. You can't always repay mentors in kind – but you can be kind ***to*** *them. Worth remembering".*

Do you have a mentor? Or do you mentor other people? Or is this a new concept for you?

HOW DO YOU DO?
Relationship skills

Most businesses need contact with other people. These may be employees, associates, suppliers, service providers, customers, clients, prospects etc. Having the skills to build effective relationships with people is an essential part of running a business.

Here are some tips on relating to people effectively:

BUILDING RELATIONSHIPS

Are you good at growing and maintaining relationships? Does this extend to your customers and clients as well as personal friends? Do you know which simple thing helps this along? These little animals do.

FRIENDLY DOGS IN THE CONSERVATORY

"Hello little dogs, how's your day been"?

"Oh, we've just been sitting here as usual, looking out of the window and admiring the garden".

"That must be relaxing. I've been quite busy this weekend trying to sort out stuff around the house and clear the decks a little".

"We don't have to do that as we don't own anything, but we do have each other, which is great".

"Yes, you obviously get on well with each other. Why do you think that is"?

"What, apart from being joined at the hip you mean"?

"Yes, what makes you stay friends after such a long time"?

"Having a common interest; that's something everyone in business should think about when they're dealing with other people".

"What do you mean exactly? What kind of common interest"?

"Well for us it's simple – we have this bone in common. We both love bones, so we spend a lot of our time chatting about it. But for business people it's about finding common ground with their colleagues, customers, clients and others. Spending some time asking questions about people's interests, ambitions, anxieties, plans, activities and so on – and, of course, listening to the answers and then chatting about some of the things you have in common – will help build your relationships. It's easy when you know what to do – and it's much more important than droning on endlessly about your own little world. Most people like it when you take an interest in them, and if you have some things in common it makes getting on with them so much easier".

"That's good to know. So tell me more about your bone................"

How do you find out people's interests?

EFFECTIVE LISTENING

Do you consider yourself to be a good listener? Have you experienced someone listening to you really well? Have you had any poor 'listening experiences'? Maybe this conversation will throw some light on the subject.

ELEPHANT ON THE BOOKCASE

"Hello elephant, you're looking thoughtful".

"Yes, I was wondering when someone would come and talk to me – it's been a while".

"Well you *are* on the top floor and I don't often need to come all the way up here, so I'm sorry if you feel neglected. Anyway, I'm here now so we can talk about what's been happening downstairs".

"That's good. I'm all ears! By the way, did you know that African elephants' ears are shaped like Africa and Indian elephants' ears are shaped like India"?

"Actually I did, but I don't know why they should be like that".

"It's because we African elephants live in very hot areas and our huge ears help protect us from the sun, as they have lots of blood vessels near the surface which cool us down. We can also use our ears as fans. But Indian elephants live in shady forests without much sunlight, so their

ears don't need to be so large. Also our ears help us hear really well – we African elephants can hear some things up to six miles away".

"Really, so does that mean you've been listening to what happens in the rest of the house, even though you're stuck up here all the time".

"Yes, absolutely; I've listened in to all your phone calls and Zoom meetings and I wish some of your business associates could listen better. I felt very sorry for you on one call a little while ago".

"Which one was that".

"The one where you'd asked someone to help you with a technical matter – and had actually paid for the advice – but it ended up with you almost having a panic attack".

"Oh yes, I remember that well".

"Well that person wasn't listening to you properly. Not taking in your questions but just thinking about information to give. And not listening to the silence either".

"What do you mean not listening to the silence"?

"When someone doesn't respond instantly, they may well be thinking and trying to process information, so if you interrupt their thoughts it can actually incapacitate them and stop any progress. That person didn't notice you were trying to absorb the information and make sense of it, but talked incessantly until it drove you mad". So listening to the silent thought processes between words is also important".

"That sounds difficult. How can you listen to silence"?

"If you can see someone, you can observe that person's body language – their eyes, their breathing and lots more – and, if in doubt, just allow them more time to respond, even if it's frustrating that they don't answer immediately. And if you can't see them – perhaps because you're on the phone, just give them enough time to formulate what they want to say".

"That's so useful. I wish more people would do that – it would make them a lot more effective and make a lot of business clients feel listened to. Thanks elephant".

Do you think you are a good listener?

EFFECTIVE COMMUNICATIONS

It's important to make sure you're saying and writing things that people can understand. See if the following is helpful.

GONG ON THE FLOOR

"Hello gong. You haven't had an outing for absolutely ages".

"Tell me about it. I've been sitting at the side of that cupboard for as long as I can remember. It's so unfair for a wonderful object such as myself. *Did you know that we gongs have been around since the Bronze Age, over 5,000 years ago, and have been used for meditation, healing and starting ceremonies, as well as communications. Some people believe that touching a gong will bring good luck, health and happiness, but it's important to have permission to approach a gong".*

"Really – I need to ask if I can talk to you; who are you trying to impress".

"Well, clearly not you; you don't seem to take me seriously. Anyway, why have you been ignoring me for so long"?

"It's mainly because I keep meaning to get a stand for you. I can hold you up to use you, but it's much easier if you're hanging somewhere accessible to start with".

"Well that's not really an excuse. I can still be used on my own, so when do you plan for me to use my voice"?

"I don't actually have a plan for that. I'm not entirely clear about how I want to use you".

"Just like lots of business owners – no idea how to use their voices either".

"What do you mean by that"?

"Well take me as an example. All you need to do is hit me with this mallet. Simple? Well not really".

"Why not".

"Because when I make a sound, it might be loud or soft, but it hardly varies apart from that".

"So"?

"So nobody listening knows what my sound means. It could be 'here's a nice sound', or 'dinner's ready', or 'emergency – react quickly'. The sound needs explaining".

"And how does that relate to business".

"Because it's important for people to make sure their voices communicate effectively, and that means being clear about the purpose of your message, using appropriate words, making sure people understand what you say and not giving conflicting messages through a difference between what you say and the 'body language' that accompanies it. Oh, and avoiding complication. Lots of business people use 'business speak, rather than plain language, which is usually unnecessary and annoying".

"And does that apply to communicating in writing as well as speech".

"Of course. You have a voice when you write, as well as when you speak, so use it well".

"Great advice gong. So how can I best use your voice"?

"I suggest you tell your next guests that when they hear me they have precisely one minute to get to the dining table. That way it will be absolutely clear what my voice (and yours) is saying".

"OK – I'll have a go at that".

"And, in the meantime, can you give me a bit of a polish? My voice is one part of my message, but my appearance backs it up – and I'd like to look professional as well as sounding it".

How about checking some of your recent communications – particularly those you've put into writing – to see if they make sense and communicate what you intended. Getting feedback on this from other people will really help.

COURTESY

What do you think of the concept of 'good manners'? Business isn't all about efficiency and cost-effectiveness; it's about treating people well too, as this little person explains.

DOORSTOP MOUSE ON THE FLOOR

"Hello mouse. What have you been up to today"?

"Oh, you know, just keeping the door open as usual".

"And has anyone interesting come through it"?

"Of course not. What a silly question; you know we haven't had guests staying here for months and months".

"True, mouse. And I don't know when it will happen again – perhaps at New Year, but I'm not holding my breath about that".

"It's a shame. I look forward to your visitors. Not only can I hold the door open for them, but I can listen to them talking and see all the things they bring with them. You know, some of them aren't very complimentary about other people they've come into contact with".

"Is that so"?

"Yes. And particularly about businesses they've had dealings with. I've heard some things that made my whiskers curl".

"So what are the worst things our visitors have talked about".

"Where do I start? Being kept on a phone line for an hour waiting for a call centre to respond; not receiving any replies to emails sent out, and receptionists not looking up to acknowledge them, despite knowing they're standing there".

"Sounds familiar. I had two pretty bad examples myself this year. The first was being told that an item missing in the post couldn't be refunded as it had gone beyond the company's time limit for complaints, despite that only happening because the company itself took several weeks to investigate the loss after I reported it. Completely unlike other companies who trust their customers and instantly send a replacement item if one is faulty or doesn't arrive".

"And the other one"?

"A delivery driver who drove a van right across the grass at the front of the house, rather than staying on the tarmac drive. It was very wet at the time and the tyres dug deep channels in the turf so we had big muddy areas for weeks until the grass started growing again. Awful".

"Well I think people who run businesses should be considerate and polite. However busy you are, it's important to consider other people's needs as much as you can. Talking of which, do you think you'd be able to get me a chunk of plastic cheese – I can't eat, but I could look at it and make myself happy".

"Of course – I'll go and look for one right now. Someone must make them – and I'll make sure to get it from the company that tries the hardest to be courteous. I'll keep you posted".

What does courtesy mean to you?

GIVING ENCOURAGEMENT

Do you know how important it is for people to feel encouraged?

LAMP IN THE KITCHEN

“Hello mirrored lamp, how are you today”.

“I’ve been thinking about the history of lamps. You know we’ve been in existence for about 70,000 years. We started off as hollow shells or rocks, which people filled with moss or similar things that they soaked in animal fat and ignited. It’s an inspirational history, but personally I’m a little uninspired today, since you ask”.

“Why’s that then”?

“I’ve not had anyone notice me today. When I’m switched on, I’m dazzling, but today I’m just sitting on the ledge and being ignored”.

“I’m so sorry, I didn’t realise you needed someone else to energise you; personally I find it easy to switch myself on”.

“Well, being a lamp, I can’t do that”.

“So what would you like me to do for you”?

"If you could just check in on me each day that would be great, and if I look a bit gloomy you can help me get going, and then I can light up your day as well as my own".

"What a great lesson lamp, and I know some team leaders who could learn from it. Thanks so much".

Do you encourage other people?

EFFECTIVE NETWORKING

Relationships are important to most businesses. And business networking is thriving – both face to face and online. Do you make the most of opportunities to meet people and grow your contacts? Maybe this will help.

GRAPES ON THE VINE

"Hello grapes. You're growing well; soon be ready to pick".

"Yes, we've had a good summer – taken advantage of the nice weather to really develop. Did you know, grapes have been around for at least 65 million years"?

"Well I'm glad you haven't yourselves – you certainly wouldn't have that lovely sheen if you were that old".

"How silly you are. We're only a few months old of course. But our closest relatives have been cultivated for 8,000 years. Most of us originated in the Middle East and there are ancient Egyptian hieroglyphics showing grapes being grown. By the way, did you know the word hieroglyph is Greek, not Egyptian, and means any form of picture writing. The Egyptian pictures showed purple grapes; we wish we were purple instead of green – it's such a lovely colour".

"Green's really lovely too though– and I also like your red neighbours a bit further along the tunnel".

"We chat quite a lot to them, you know. It's so much more interesting when you can meet others and find out about them and share ideas. That's how we found out about the hieroglyphics – the red grapes told us. Apparently they'd heard it on the radio in here – we must have been taking a nap at the time so we didn't hear the programme".

"Didn't realise you all talked to each other".

"Of course, we do – we don't just hang about, you know. It's a great way to pass the time and everyone benefits. It's a bit like what you humans do – but you call it networking. We hear that's got very popular nowadays".

"Yes, it has, but I'm surprised to hear you talk about it".

"Well we do catch up with some of the programmes on the radio in our polytunnel – we're not asleep ***all*** *the time - and lots of them seem to feature networking. Did you know it can really help grow your business by extending your contacts, developing new relationships, promoting what you do and developing your skills".*

"Developing your skills - really"?

"Yes, you get the opportunity to practise listening well, improve how you communicate, do some presenting, learn how other people promote their businesses, improve your memory and increase your confidence – invaluable".

"Well, you're certainly good at networking – look at all of you on one bunch, and then getting together with different bunches all over the place. We humans could certainly take a leaf out of your book".

"Take a leaf off our vine, we think you mean. Thanks for the compliment".

How important is networking to your own business and have you already learned any networking skills?

PRESENTATION SKILLS

Do you ever need to make a presentation – either face to face or through video-conferencing? If so, do you enjoy it, or does the thought fill you with dread? Here are some ideas from a large object.

FLIP CHART ON THE RADIATOR

"Hello flip chart, so sorry to put you up here on the radiator, but I just wanted to wipe you down".

"How wonderful. Does that mean we're going somewhere today"?

"Yes – it's our first outing for ages. We're going to give a talk to a lovely group of people in a village hall".

"That's exciting - much better than being stuck away behind a chair in a room that's hardly used. I thought I'd never come out again".

"You and me both, but here we are, about to go".

"What are we talking about today".

"How to use your mind more effectively".

"Talking about a personal problem, are we"?

"How rude. No, it's helping people understand they can do things better than they may think".

"Well I hope you extend that to some of your colleagues; from what I've heard some of them could do with a few tips about presentating".

"I could certainly do that - but let's test *your* knowledge. You've been involved in lots of presentations; what do *you* think are the most important things for a presenter to do".

"Hmmm. There are quite a few I can tell you about. By the way, did you know flip charts have been in existence for over 100 years and I think we're still useful – so much more personal than those automated systems. I've heard of death by Powerpoint, but never death by flipchart – unless one of us fell on your head, of course".

"Yes, thanks for the history lesson, but what about those tips".

"Well, firstly prepare well and know what you're going to talk about. Be sure to include the essentials and have a few topics to leave out or add in if time is short or you finish early. Find out about your audience in advance and start to build good relationships by chatting with one or two of them before you start. Appear confident by moving around a bit and seeming comfortable with the space you have. Look at people when you're speaking, vary your expressions and tone of voice and answer questions appropriately. And wear interesting clothes (even if it's just a colourful tie or scarf), to give people something to focus on while you're speaking. Remember you don't have to know absolutely everything about your subject – it's OK to say you don't know and you'll find out. And, finally, remember to breathe – it's really useful (not that I'd know about that personally, of course)".

"Thanks flipchart – I'll bear all that in mind".

When was the last time you used a flip chart? And have you been to any 'death by Powerpoint' presentations?

LEADERSHIP SKILLS

What do you think constitutes good leadership? Do you believe you are a good leader? What would you teach someone just stepping up into a leadership position. Maybe this little pig could help out.

PIG CONDUCTOR ON THE CUPBOARD

"Hello conductor. Your little band looks very cheerful".

"They always love their music and they make a great team".

"Well you're obviously doing a good job of keeping them on track".

"No more than any good leader should do. But I'm sure you've come across some humans who aren't brilliant at leading a team".

"Yes, you're right. Some are great but I've met a few who are truly dreadful. What do you think makes you good as a conductor"?

"I've never thought about that before, but I suppose there are a few things that are important to me, although others may think differently".

"I'd be really interested to hear your opinion".

"Well here's what I think is important. Be self-aware, build good relationships with members of your team; understand that everyone has their own way of functioning so you may need to adapt to that when necessary, listen well, agree challenging but achievable targets, notice if things are going wrong, help anyone having difficulties, praise good work and set a good example".

"That's a great list, conductor. It certainly keeps your band on their toes"!

"Yes, pigs have to be on their toes to play musical instruments of course. By the way, did you know that conducting has quite a long history. In the middle ages, hand gestures were used a lot, particularly in chanting, to indicate the rise and fall of a melody. But I don't think a lot of that was done by pigs like me".

"No, I don't think so either.

What principles do you think are important in leadership?

HAVE A SUPPORT GROUP

Do you love working alone or do you need others to support you? Maybe these little dogs can help.

SINGING DOGS ON THE SHELF

"Hello dogs – lovely to see you again. Has it really been a year since you had an outing"?

Yes, last Christmas; can't believe it ourselves. And it's great to have the other animals around too – the little white dog, the reindeer, the bears, the birds and even the cat! And we're so pleased there are three of us together all the time".

"Why particularly"?

"Because it would be rather lonely if it was each one of us individually. We're just like some of your business colleagues; they run their businesses on their own, but they also have other people they can call on for support".

"Very true. Sometimes it's others working by themselves, sometimes it's people doing the same kind of work, sometimes it's family or friends and sometimes it's just people online or on social media who can comment on ideas, commiserate when things go wrong, cheer you up when you're having a hard day and congratulate you when you've been successful".

"And for us it's others to share our song and keep us on key. Did you know carols were first sung in Europe thousands of years ago, but they were pagan songs, sung at the winter solstice, not Christmas carols. And the word 'Carol' means a joyful or festive song, or dance in a ring, accompanied by singers. So you should be good at singing – but you really aren't! We're much better, although not everyone likes to hear dogs singing, which really surprises us".

"Yes, strange that, but humans have different thoughts about what makes for a good tune. Mind you, you've had years and years of practising that one song. I can see the notes on the other side of your music sheet, so it's not surprising you're pretty good by now".

"Tell that to the reindeer – it always has its nose in the air when it sees us, although we do catch it trying out some of our song when it doesn't think we're listening".

"So it's benefitting from you, even though it doesn't realise it. Just like some people – don't like to let on they need anyone else, but if you offer help they might well be really grateful. Must spread the word on that one. Thanks dogs".

"You're welcome – now where are our treats"?

Do you have a support network you can rely on?

WHERE DO I START?
Business processes

There are some skills that specifically relate to running a business. Many, of course, are also used in other contexts as well, but most businesses can benefit from the ones that follow.

ENTREPRENEURSHIP

Are you happy with your motivation, your branding, your USP? Did you need a leg-up when you started out on your own? Here's a tale of initiative.

LITTLE PLANT ON THE TABLE

"Hello little plant, what's happened to you? It looks as if you've had an accident and fallen out of your pot".

"Thanks for your concern, but it's intentional. I've been thinking about it for ages and decided the time had come to separate myself from the competition".

"Pardon"?

"There were so many of us in that pot and I never stood out. Anyone looking at us would think we were all the same, but I knew I was different and could make more of myself. So I jumped ship, as I think you refer to it".

"Well that's interesting, but what were you hoping to achieve"?

"I wanted to show what I could do. You humans do exactly the same, or at least some of you do. While most people seem happy working for someone else, some set out on their own to run a business. It's been reported that there are almost 600 million entrepreneurs in the world – about 5% of the total population. Also, second incomes are on the rise, with at least a quarter, and possibly many more, of the working population of the UK having a secondary income. This is most common with millennnials – almost 80% of people aged between 25 and 34 currently have some kind of 'side hustle'. And podcasting is the most lucrative, while the most popular is selling some kind of handmade items. But even with all those business ventures, many of you don't show your customers or clients how you are unique and so they don't understand why they should come to you, rather than anyone else".

"You're right, little plant; I've noticed that myself. And nowadays, with so many people working for themselves, it's even more important to stand out from the crowd. So that's what you're doing – very clever".

"Well, almost very clever. I hate to admit it, but I can't do it all by myself. As you can see, I'm stuck on this table and I really need a pot of my own to flourish in. Do you think you could help me"?

"Certainly. Some of us humans spend a lot of time helping new little businesses flourish and learn the ropes, so helping you into a new pot will be easy peasy. Just tell me where you'd like to start".

"That sunny windowsill would be great. Everyone can see me there and I'll be able to raise my profile and become a healthy big plant. Who knows, with time I might even help a few other little plants establish themselves as well - once I'm on my way".

"Sounds great – just let me go and find a pot that will suit you and we can make a start".

How well do you think you are suited to running a business of your own? And do you understand the requirements in terms of aptitude, skills and temperament?

CHOOSE SOMETHING YOU ENJOY

If you're running a business (or even if you're doing a job), it's important for it to be something you enjoy. See if you agree with the sentiments this object expresses.

CANDLE HOLDER ON THE SHELF

"Hello candle holder, you look cheerful".

"I'm always cheerful. I love holding my candle and looking down at everything going on in the kitchen. I love listening to people's conversations. I love watching you cook. I'm always happy".

"I'm so pleased for you; it's great to enjoy life".

"Of course. But so many people in business don't seem to enjoy their lives very much, which is sad".

"Why do you think that is"?

"Because they aren't doing something they're really passionate about. People who are successful can't wait to start work each day and they love their activities and the benefits they, and their customers or clients, get from them".

"But not everyone can have the luxury of doing something they enjoy".

"I know. Sometimes you humans have to accept work that's tedious, or hard, or unrewarding. But very often people don't think enough before starting out and they could have made different choices had they been better informed".

"I suppose that's true. Not everyone gets good career advice, and some people just go into business because they think they'll make money, rather than because what they're doing has much meaning for them. They don't have any emotional connection with their work and it becomes just a means to an end, rather than enjoyable in itself".

"Well look at me. I have very limited activity – in fact, now I come to think of it, I have no activity at all unless I fall off this shelf. But I've found enjoyable things around me which keep me amused and interested every day. I'm very grateful, because I didn't have a choice. I think your business associates should review, periodically, what they're doing and make sure they really do want to be doing it".

"And if they don't"?

"Then they need a plan B. They should work out a way of making changes so they have a more rewarding work life. Otherwise they're destined to spend years and years regretting things they never did".

"That's not a cheerful thought is it"?

"No, it isn't. But while they're doing things they don't enjoy much, there are ways of staying cheerful. One great thing is to make sure their bodies produce lots of 'happy hormones'. Then they can stay brighter while they're changing their work lives for the better".

"Do tell me more about those hormones".

"There's serotonin, which helps with positive moods and good sleep. You can increase seratonin by getting outside and letting the daylight help you feel better (or even have an artificial light that mimics daylight, which is the next best thing). Exercise also helps you produce serotonin – even a quick walk will do it. And having a good diet helps too. Then there's oxytocin, which also helps you feel happy. Physical contact with other people often helps increase this, which is why a hug can make you feel good, and so can stroking an animal. Endorphins can help you feel great (and also reduce pain) and they can be encouraged through exercise, eating dark chocolate and spicy food (not necessarily together), having a massage and laughing. And then there's dopamine which helps with pleasure, motivation and focus – and you can increase

dopamine by doing things you enjoy including celebrations and having treats".

"Well that's quite a list – lots of things to do".

"Yes, but some people can get all that from their work anyway. Just imagine – if you were a personal trainer, who ran classes outdoors in the daylight and also offered a massage service. All you'd need then would be an occasional treat and you'd have all four of those hormones covered. Worth thinking about. And, while we're talking about cheerfulness, perhaps you'd give my candle a bit of a dust – it would look even better if it was clean and would make me much happier".

Are you doing something you love in your work life?

DO YOUR RESEARCH

If you haven't yet started a business, or are thinking of diversifying, it's important to check if there's interest in, or a need for, what you intend to provide.

MAGNIFYING GLASS IN THE DESK

"Hello magnifying glass. Not used you for a long time".

"I thought I hadn't seen you recently. In fact I wondered if I still had a purpose here, which is sad as glasses like me have a very long history".

"Really"?

"Yes, you know the ancient Egyptians used chips of crystal, or shiny stones, to see small objects better. And apparently the Emperor Nero used to look at things through glass or stones and it was said he 'got a better view of an actress by looking at her through a gemstone'"!

"Well I didn't know that. But I do know you're really useful and you were invaluable when I needed to check things out in detail – maybe looking at an old photograph, or reading tiny instructions on products, but since I started wearing varifocals it's much easier to do that kind of thing".

"You know it's not only physical items that need checking out".

"Really – what do you have in mind"?

"I was thinking about people who want to set up a new business – they need to check things out too".

"Do give me some examples".

"Well they should find out if anyone wants or needs what they're thinking of offering. No point in providing something that doesn't have a use. Of course the opposite is sometimes true as well. If it's a very crowded marketplace it might not be sensible to set yourself up where there's a huge amount of competition – unless what you're doing is very distinctive, of course".

"I see. And what else might people need to check out"?

"How much it might cost to produce products and whether they'd need financial backing, what level of sales would be required to give a sensible return, what expertise they might need to acquire to operate effectively, whether the market they're thinking of entering is stable or volatile – there are all kinds of things to consider".

"So you're saying it's important to do your research before you start".

"Absolutely. Use a magnifying glass to check out the details and maybe use my friend the torch to shine a light on areas that may not be clear to start with".

"Thanks magnifying glass – didn't realise the torch was your friend".

"Yes – we go back a long way – just like you".

"Cheek"!

What research could you do when considering a new venture?

LOCATION

How do you decide where your business will be based?

GARDEN BENCH ON THE LAWN

"Hello garden bench; you're looking very wintery today".

"Yes. Not often we get snow nowadays, so it's nice to see something different".

"At least you're still upright. You've completely blown over in some of the strong winds we've had in the past".

"I know. Not nice to keep falling on your back – although I suppose it's better than falling flat on your face"!

"Well we do our best to keep you looking good and I bought you a lovely new green seat cover last year although, now I come to think about it, it never saw the light of day; I must remember to get it out for you when the weather next improves".

"That would be good. You know benches used to be very commonplace in the days when chairs were reserved for important people, but you don't see us indoors very often".

"That's because you're large and heavy and wouldn't fit into most people's houses. Certainly couldn't be moved about easily".

"That can't be said about businesses though".

"What can't be said about businesses"?

"That they can't be moved. Nowadays businesses can move pretty much anywhere at the speed of light. They might choose to have physical locations, or they could go online and operate globally without stepping outside their own front doors".

"Very different from when I was young. We had quill pens and an abacus you know".

"Now who's being silly"!

What ideas do you have about where you will work from and where your customers might be based?

WORKING ENVIRONMENT

Do you pay attention to your working environment? Maybe this little mat can help.

BATHMAT ON THE FLOOR

"Hello little bathmat. You're looking very pretty".

"Well thank you. I don't get noticed all that often as I have such a low profile".

"Yes – you couldn't have a much lower one if you tried. Nonetheless you are really useful – I couldn't do without you. It's so much more comfortable stepping out of the bath onto something soft – although the carpet under you would do if it had to".

"Be careful – it might be listening; don't want to offend it. My guess is that not everyone thinks of comfort – particularly at work; but that's where it's really important".

"In what way"?

"If you don't have a comfortable chair, good lighting, the right height desk, somewhere to rest your wrists and enough air coming through it could affect your health. And of course the same applies if you're not working in an office; whatever your workplace it's important to think about comfort. You know there's a word for all that – ergonomics. That word was first featured in a story in 1857 and the real study of ergonomics came from looking at machines, such as aircraft, where it was found that many crashes seemed to be the result of poor design features relating to the human body".

"So are you saying that if you're comfortable at work, you could feel better, use your body more effectively and be more productive".

"Exactly. So me being here on your bathroom floor is helping you run your business better".

"That could be a slight exaggeration – my bathroom isn't a place of work".

"I disagree. I hear you muttering about ideas that have come to you and I see you writing them down once you've come out of the bath. If that isn't work, what is"?

"OK – you do have a point. So let's see if the tax people will let me put you down as a business expense".

"Good luck with that"!

Is your working environment suitable for your needs?

HAVING A RANGE OF ACTIVITIES

Does your business specialise in one thing to the exclusion of all others? Do you have a small number of activities? Or do you have lots of strands to what you do? Perhaps it's a topic worth exploring....

HATS ON THE CUPBOARD

"Hello hats. You're looking a trifle dusty".

"A trifle? More like a whole dessert course. Nobody's come near us for months, if not years. We feel most neglected".

"Sorry. I do like hats. But I really don't like wearing them. I prefer to admire them from a distance".

"Why's that"?

"Wearing a hat squashes my hair down so that it's completely flat. And hats also give me a headache, so I rarely wear one. But I really should have paid you a bit more attention. Trouble is you seem a bit out of reach for me, being so high up on the cupboard".

"That's not a great excuse. But at least you know you have us. So many business people have only one hat and they don't realise there's a

whole world of hats out there – and well within their reach - if they only took the time to explore".

"And why would they need more than one hat? They only have one head each"!

"That's missing the point; we were speaking metaphorically (or should that be hataphorically)? If you only wear one business hat you have all your eggs in one basket (oh dear, another hataphor). But if you have a few business hats then you have a few income streams; a few different interests; a few options should the financial climate, or your personal circumstances, change)".

"Yes, I see. But not everyone is good at lots of things".

"Maybe not lots, but certainly some. Given today's economic climate, pace of change and consumer capriciousness, wearing different hats is a good insurance policy. And also a remedy for boredom. Wish ***we*** *had one of those".*

"Wish you had one of what"?

"A remedy for boredom. We're stuck up on this cupboard with nothing to entertain us apart from the birds we hear through the window – and we can't even see them because we're facing a different direction. At least take us down occasionally and admire us – we have a long history you know. The first hat was seen in a cave painting in France and was dated 15,000 years BC. London black cabs were made tall so that men could ride in them without taking off their top hats and chefs' tall hats traditionally have 100 pleats to represent hundreds of ways an egg can be prepared".

"I didn't know all of that. Clearly having a variety of hats adds spice to life, and also business. Worth knowing".

How many business hats do YOU wear?

PLANNING

Do you ever find yourself on a bit of a hamster wheel? Do you sometimes find it hard to structure a project? Do you occasionally find it difficult to keep your end goal in mind? Hope this helps.

WOODEN SCULPTURE ON THE MANTELPIECE

"Hello curly sculpture. I'm trying to work out where you begin and end".

"That's a pointless exercise with me, I'm afraid. I don't have a beginning or an end, or a middle even. I'm just one continuous stream".

"Actually that's rather nice. Sounds very relaxing – you just circle around endlessly without having to get anywhere".

"You've got it. Yes, I really enjoy that; it's a relaxed way to live. Of course, it's no use whatsoever in business".

"What do you mean"?

"Well, a business needs to be profitable. So its owner has to do things effectively".

"That goes without saying, doesn't it"?

"No, I don't think so. Lots of business owners do exactly what I do; they go around in circles without ever reaching an end point. And they sometimes get stuck in the middle of a project, because they don't know how to move forward, or they get distracted from the task in hand".

"That sounds familiar; I've done some of that myself. I've found I jump into things without a real objective, or a clear plan, so I have no way of monitoring how successful I'm being. What would you suggest to improve things".

"Well, as a piece of wood, of course I'm no expert, but I think it would be good to know what you want to achieve, decide on a start date and plan out some specific steps towards your goal. That way you can always measure how far you are along your path and make sure you're actually doing things that will get the results you want".

"That sounds very simple".

"Well what did you expect from me – rocket science?

What stops you being productive? Do you plan your activities? Do you have any measures of success?

STRATEGIC PLANNING

Does your business just bat along from day to day, or do you have a strategic plan for its future? Maybe it's all about playing a game.

CHESS SET ON THE COFFEE TABLE

"Hello chess set – your pieces are looking as elegant as ever. Shame nobody plays with them".

"I think so too. We have a history going back about 1500 years, but you only bought us because you liked the gold Afghan hounds".

"True – reminded me of our own Afghans and how stunning they were. I haven't played chess since I was at school, and none of our visitors seem to have expressed a desire to do so either. It's a pity you've been neglected, but then chess never really was my thing".

"That's crystal clear, but then strategic thinking isn't really your strong point either, is it"?

"What do you mean"?

"Well chess involves strategy, just like business, but you seem to get by without it".

"Do you really think so? I was quite pleased with myself the other year, when I decided to launch three books for Christmas and also do a few other major things as well. I scheduled them in and then stuck to my schedule so I got them done".

*"**Almost** got them done, you mean; one got left behind".*

"I know, but time ran out".

"I heard that time runs out at the beginning of a project, not the end, so if you don't plan and organise things properly from the start then you may not get them finished".

"You're right, but surely that's not about strategy".

"No, but strategy and tactics both go hand in hand. Not much point in doing one of them without the other. When people play with my chess pieces I can tell immediately if they have a strategy for the game and, if they don't, then there's nowhere for the tactics to sit comfortably and their results aren't good, unless it's by pure chance".

"Well I'm sorry you get disappointed".

"Me too, but at least I don't lose money or struggle because of it. Unlike businesses which don't have a strategy. Worth remembering. And so are we – please tell your friends we're just waiting to be played with, when they want a break from all that work they're doing".

"I certainly will. It's my next move".

Do you have a strategy for your business? And, if not, why is that?

SUPPLY CHAIN AND PRODUCTION

How can you ensure you get the resources you need for your business to function?

DRIED LIMES ON THE TABLE

"Hello dried limes – there's a wonderful scent coming from your container".

"Yes – we may be dried, but we're still full of goodness. We originated in the Middle East, where we're often called black limes. Over there, we're dried in the sun and used to give a slightly sour taste to some dishes".

"I thought I'd put you in some soup for lunch. It's such a relief to know you're there in the food cupboard in case we can't get any fresh limes".

"It's not usually difficult to get limes, but we're glad you've planned ahead. Lots of businesses that are involved in production and sales often forget about their supply chain until it's too late".

"What do you mean"?

"Well tangible goods have components and these often come from different places. For example, suppose you make jam. You may well have fruit trees in a garden or orchard, but you also need sugar to make the jam, and may also need pectin or flavourings, which you're unlikely to produce yourself. So they have to come from somewhere else. A supply chain is really all the stages required for the end result and it may include producers, importers, warehousing, distribution and much more".

"But if I made jam I wouldn't need all of those".

"You might. For example, you would need jars – where would they come from. And labels – where would they come from. And sugar – where would that come from? And each of those will have a production source and possibly an importer or distributor and so on. It's all quite complex".

"And what's all that got to do with you, limes"?

"Well you decided to make us yourself from fresh limes because we taste good, but also in case you couldn't get fresh limes later on. Businesses need to consider what would happen if their supplies were put at risk, and make provision for that situation. It's just good management of resources".

"And I thought I was just making a nice preserve – you live and learn"!

What supply chain issues might your business have?

CHECK YOUR FINANCES

Are you on top of your incomings and outgoings? If not, you might run into problems.

SPIRIT LEVEL IN THE BASEMENT

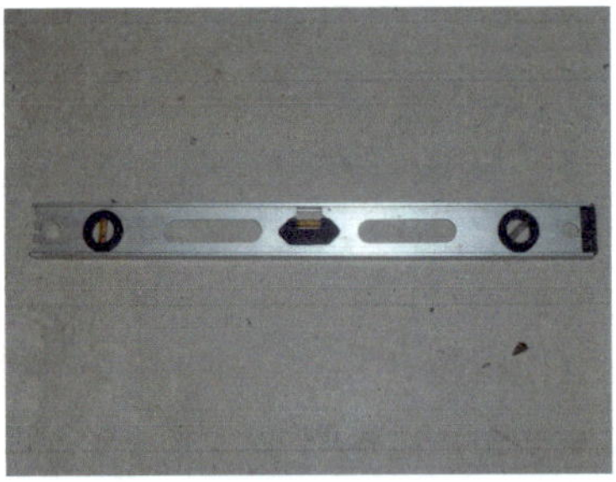

"Hello spirit level. Glad you're still around. Nothing I like less than a shelf or picture or other object that isn't correctly positioned".

"I know. I remember when you had a new kitchen put in and told the fitters the hob wasn't parallel with the front of the worktop".

"Yes, and they had the nerve to argue with me until we measured it and found it was a couple of millimetres out".

"You don't think that's nit-picky then"?

"I certainly do not. Especially if you're dealing with people who are paid large amounts of money to get their measurements right".

"And they do have us spirit levels to help them, of course. You know we were invented around 1660, although lots of builders still preferred to fill old bottles with water and use them in a similar way. We measure how parallel or perpendicular a surface is relative to the earth and we're generally filled with coloured alcohol, which is why the word spirit is used".

"Well I didn't think it was to do with the supernatural".

"Silly – of course not, although it would be quite funny if you were haunted by a spirit level, given your predilection for accuracy. But diverging slightly, I think we could be quite useful in financial matters".

"How so"?

"By helping people work out their finances. If they put me on top of their piles of invoices and receipts – one at each end, then they could easily see whether they were getting more money in than was going out – or vice versa".

"I don't think it's as simple as that. You can't just stack up your financial records and assume they're equal, but if you're trying to say that businesses should be aware of whether they're running profitably or not, then that *is* an important point".

"Yes, that was exactly what I meant. Being able to see easily whether you're in debt, or making a good return. I'm sure we could help".

"Sorry to disappoint you, but there are computer systems and accountants to do that nowadays. You're a bit behind the times. But since you originated almost four hundred years ago I'll cut you some slack".

"And I'll do the same for you as you're rapidly catching me up - grins".

Are you on top of your own finances?

CASH FLOW

Income producing activities are great, but it's important for that income to arrive in good time, as these little individuals explain.

CORN COBS IN THE CONSERVATORY

"Hello corn cobs; you're always a cheerful bunch".

"Yes, we are, although we're sad to have lost our bright colours. When we were young we were blue and pink and purple and orange and yellow and red and really stood out against the stone wall".

"So you were; I'd forgotten that. I just had to take you home with me when I saw you in the shop and you looked great for ages and ages. Actually you still look great – more mature, more elegant – a bit like me".

"Kind of you to say so, but did you know corn isn't just decorative or edible? Some of us have even been used as money".

"No, I don't think I knew that".

"Yes, in America for example, in the seventeenth century, we were used by settlers as money and to trade for meat and furs. We were known as commodity money, like salt, shells, decorative belts and peppercorns. And corn, together with wheat, peas, beef, butter and other things was

sometimes called 'pay', or 'country pay', so we have a really interesting history".

"I didn't learn about that sort of money in school".

"No, and lots of business people don't even learn enough about money to keep their businesses going".

"How do you mean".

"Well it's not just important for your business to produce income; that income needs to arrive in time for you to pay your bills; we think you humans refer to that process as cash flow".

"Actually, you've reminded me of something. Many years ago I ran an employment agency with a friend, but the hospitals we supplied with locum staff didn't pay us for months and, in the end, we had to wind up the business. It was really successful, and had a great reputation, but we couldn't afford to pay the staff we supplied because of those late payments to us".

"Exactly. When your income arrives is as important as how much you earn. If you can't pay your bills you go out of business. Luckily, there are lots of things you can do to avoid that situation, such as requesting payment within a set number of days, adding an additional few per cent on for late payment, or finding someone to act as a debt collector for you".

"And to think I just came in here to sit down for five minutes and I got lessons in history and economics as well. I'll never underestimate corn cobs again. Thanks very much".

Have you ever had cash flow issues with your business?

'HANDS-ON' EXPERIENCE

Are you familiar with all aspects of your business? Or do you hesitate to take on some tasks which seem too basic for your expertise? Maybe you could lower your sights a little from time to time.

GARDENING GLOVES ON THE BOILER

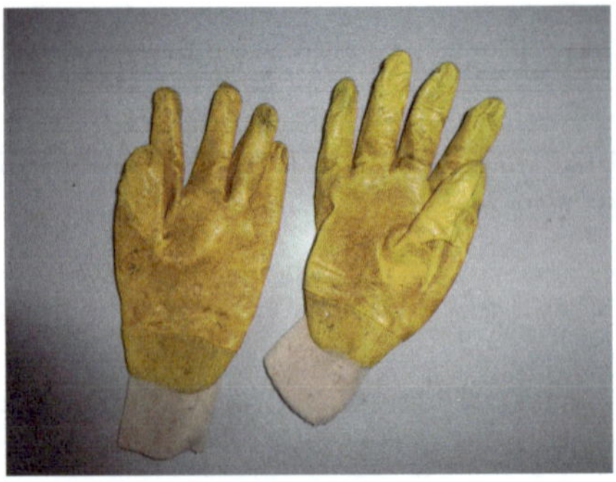

"Hello gardening gloves, let's put in a few more little plants while the weather's good".

"That would be nice. We've not been out for a while because of the rain, so it's good to get some fresh air again. What are we putting in today?"

"I thought we'd plant some Lupin Tree seedlings, as they're outgrowing their pots. It may take a bit of time though, as the ground I want to put them in is very hard and there are lots of big stones in it – I bent the fork last time I tried digging there".

"Yes, we remember that outing; let's hope it's a bit easier today. But why do you need to wear us all the time? The famous gardeners on TV don't ever wear gloves – are your hands so much more tender than theirs"?

"Don't know, but I certainly don't like getting them covered in earth, or scratched by brambles, or irritated by horrible plants that stick to you all the time".

"How feeble is that. So you're telling us that you don't like getting your hands dirty. What would it be like if all your business colleagues behaved like that"?

"What, wore gloves while gardening"?

"No, you shouldn't take everything so literally. We mean that, if you run a business, you can't do it all from a distance. You have to get stuck into things, even if you sometimes think it's beneath you to do it. When you've experienced all aspects of your business, you have a much better feel for how it works – and that's particularly important if it's a large business and there are areas you know little about. If you don't know

what your staff actually do, it's harder to lead or encourage them, so getting ground-level experience where possible makes you better informed and able to make decisions based on real understanding rather than theoretical concepts".

"I suppose that's true. Only the other day I heard a talk by the CEO of a huge organisation, who had taken over its management from his father, who founded it. The son said his father insisted he start 'at the bottom', by sweeping floors in warehouses, before moving on to other areas of the business. By the time he took over he had a real understanding of how it all worked, and that wouldn't have been the same if he'd just stepped in at the top with no hands-on experience".

"See, you do know what we're talking about. So how about some 'hands-on' – or rather 'gloves-off' - experience yourself now? Just for five minutes, leave us on the ground and have a go without us. You might even enjoy it".

Do you have 'hands on' experience of all of your business? And, if not, why not?

KNOW YOUR COMPETITION

How much do you know about your competitors (if you have any – and most of us do, of course)? Why should you bother to find out? Maybe these little utensils can throw some light on the subject.

COOKING SET ON THE WORKTOP

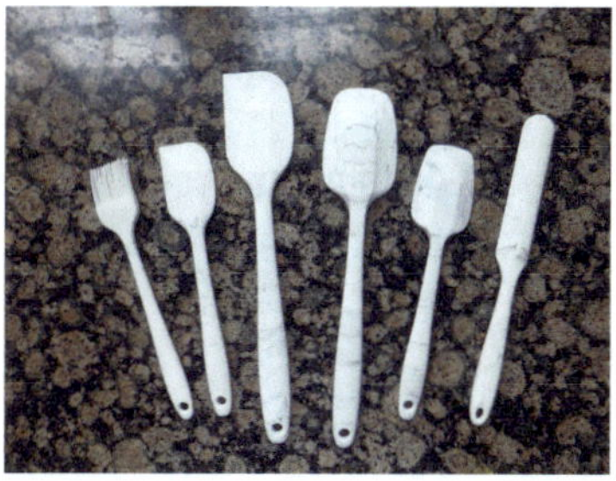

"Hello cooking set, you look a nice addition to my kitchen".

"Thank you so much; we're pleased to be here".

"I was a bit surprised to see you all – some of you look quite similar to each other".

"Well we're not really. We may look the same, but if you take the time to look carefully, we're actually all different. A bit like competitors in business, you know".

"Oh, more business advice from inanimate objects! I thought maybe, as you were new, you wouldn't be as mouthy as my existing artefacts, but clearly I was wrong".

"We're so underestimated. Everybody thinks that, just because we aren't human, we don't know anything, but we have all the time in the world to take in information while we're sitting around for hours, days, weeks or months waiting to be used".

"I suppose that's true. So why are you like business competitors then"?

*"Well, in business, you have to have something to differentiate yourself from everyone else. That might be your product range, your support services, your speed of delivery and, of course, you as the business owner. As someone (probably **not** Oscar Wilde) said: 'Be yourself, everyone else is taken' ".*

"But you still haven't told me why all of *you* are like business competitors".

*"Oh dear, you're slow on the uptake, aren't you. **We** are all different. Although we serve similar purposes, some of us are large and some are small; some are round and some are pointy, some are rigid and some are more flexible. **Each** of us is different in some way, so if you find your own points of difference – business people call them USPs, or unique selling points, you'll be able to promote your services to buyers more effectively".*

"Thanks so much, cooking set. My business skills will be much improved now".

"Unlike your cooking!"

"I HEARD THAT".

What's your own USP?

MARKETING

Marketing is the life blood of business. If nobody knows about you then your products or services are unlikely to sell.

SHOPPING BAG ON THE DOOR HANDLE

"Hello shopping bag; you're being very patient there".

"Well I have to be. Now you get your supermarket shopping delivered each week I hardly ever have an outing. I miss those trips out of the house".

"So sorry, but I can't just go out in order to please you".

"But I was made to go to market – I'm wasted if I don't do it. Like your business associates who produce wonderful goods and services, but don't let people know about them – that's about going to market too, you know".

"Not quite in the same way as you though".

"No, but that's not the point. You know people have been marketing things for thousands of years. Branding was seen in ancient Rome 2,000 years ago. One example was a mosaic floor decorated with illustrations of containers with fish sauce produced by a particular individual, whose reputation spread across much of the Mediterranean. So even back then people understood about marketing".

"Well that's all well and good, but your trip to market will have to wait – I have other things to do today".

"Spoilsport"!

How much do you do in the way of marketing for your business"?

POP UPS FOR MARKETING

Is your business a traditional one? Do you always have the same offerings, or have you ventured into anything new. Here are some ideas from an unlikely source.

GRASS BLADES IN THE UTILITY ROOM

"Hello adventitious blades of grass. You weren't here last week".

"Hello yourself. No, we weren't. But all those pumpkins you put on the drainer straight from the field dropped earth into the sink and we found it and – well – just popped up".

"So I see. It's not an obvious place for you though, is it? If you stay there your future's likely to be limited. Wouldn't you be better off in the lawn"?

"Probably, but it's quite fun experimenting and finding out how people react. You know lots of businesses work like that nowadays".

"Do they"?

"Yes, we heard it on the radio the other day. Lots of them have pop ups apparently. They might be little temporary shops, online events, dining

clubs, flash mobs – all kinds of things. They're good ways of trying out new products or locations and getting a buzz around what a business does. Speaking of which, do you think you could open the window and let out that wasp that's been buzzing around us all morning. Getting attention is great, but we'd rather it wasn't from a wasp".

"Yes, I can do that. Here you go wasp, fly out and join the others in the garden. So you're saying pop ups can be a good way of marketing what you do".

"And also a good way of making extra money without investing in permanent venues or staffing. People have dined in a field, or in a container suspended on a crane. Arts organisations have held impromptu performances in railway stations.
You can go to where your customers are, rather than having them come to you. And keeping the location secret until the last minute can create lots of anticipation".

"That all sounds good. What do you think is the most interesting pop up you've heard of"?

"Has to be the Japanese pancake company which wanted to show people how nutritious its products were. They opened a pop up shop which had clear tubes on the walls showing the nutrients that most fast food lacked. They let visitors swap receipts from other fast food outlets for little phials which contained the nutrients missing from the meals they'd had. Then they posted a video online and their business increased enormously".

"That's a great initiative. Will have to think what I can do in the way of pop-ups. But it won't be growing more plants in the kitchen sink".

Have you experimented with pop ups in your business?

SALES

Are you good at selling or are you one of those people who think 'sales' is a rude word? Selling is NOT about 'persuading' people to buy stuff they don't want – so let's see what it really is.

FRYING PAN ON THE HOB

"Hello frying pan – you're looking very shiny today".

"I've just been in the dish washer and come out looking good as new. What are we going to do today"?

"We have some visitors coming for lunch, so I'll need you to help me feed them".

"Easy peasy – that's my job".

"But I don't know whether they'll like what I give them".

"That's a common problem in business you know. People don't know how to assess their customers".

"What exactly do you mean"?

"Well let's take you as an example; what might you say to your visitors beforehand"?

"I suppose I'd say I'm going to do a nice lunch".

"And who do you expect to think it's nice"?

"Well them, of course".

"But you haven't asked them what they enjoy – or even what they dislike. How do you expect to please them if you don't know what they like to eat".

"Good point, frying pan. So I could say I'm going to cook fish and see what they say".

"You could, but it would be better to ask them specifically what their preferences are".

"Yes – of course; you're right. Personally I love plaice but can't bear haddock and I wouldn't want to give them the wrong thing".

"So then you could go a bit further".

"What – tell them it will be fried in butter"?

"No, that's what's called a feature – something about the item. You want to tell them what eating your fish will give them".

"It'll give them a full stomach, I hope".

"Not quite what I mean. You could tell them it will taste delicious, help them keep their calorie intake down, be a novel dining experience and give them something to tell their friends about afterwards".

"In other words the reasons for them enjoying the meal".

"You've got it. Now, shall we get on".

"But what am I going to make for the visitors"?

"I dunno – you're the cook"!

Do you effectively promote the benefits of your products or services to potential customers or clients?

CUSTOMER CARE

Do you have customers or clients? If so, do you know how to treat them well – and why it's important to do so? We've all probably had experiences of good, and bad, customer service, so it's worth taking some time to get yours up to scratch.

MENU-HOLDER IN THE CUPBOARD

"Hello menu-holder. Just spotted you on the top shelf. I'd almost forgotten you existed".

"Well thank you so much. I thought you'd been busy, but you're obviously simply not bothered about my feelings".

"I'm really sorry; I didn't mean to upset you. But it's been almost two years since we had enough people over to use your services. I really only need to produce a list of food at gatherings when I've made lots of options".

"I know that, but even when you do write a menu you don't always think properly about your customers".

"My friends aren't customers – they come over to have a meal and a chat".

"Yes, but if you thought of them as customers you might take a different approach".

"Please explain what you mean by that".

"Well, instead of just writing the names of dishes, you might list some of the ingredients, or whether they're suitable for vegetarians, or if they're hot or cold, or if you need a fork or a spoon to eat them".

"Is that really necessary, menu-holder? Surely people can work that out for themselves".

"They could, but if they were actually paying customers, wouldn't you want to give them all the information they need to make a decision. And

also let them know what to do if they don't like it, perhaps, or if they'd like something completely different".

"Well wouldn't they just stop eating if they didn't like it"?

"They might, but some people feel obliged to finish everything on their plate, whether they like it or not".

"Yes, I've heard that, although I never had that message myself as a child".

"This is all about taking on the perspective of other people. Think of their point of view and then you can offer great service both before and after they buy from you. It really pays off".

"Thanks menu-holder; let's hope we can put this into practice before too long".

What's the best, or worst, customer service you've received?

UNTAPPED BUSINESS RESOURCES

Do you know you probably have untapped resources in your business? This encounter may throw some light on that fact.

COBWEB ON THE STAIRCASE

"Hello cobweb. You're very cosy there".

"Oooooooooooooooooh; you spotted me! I thought I'd made myself inconspicuous".

"Actually you had, but the sunlight from the big window showed you up".

"Pleeeeeeeease don't sweep me up; I'm not doing anyone any harm".

"Well I did think about moving you on; what can you say to persuade me not to"?

"If I tell you how your business could make better use of resources, would you let me stay here"?

"Business advice from a cobweb; that's got to be a first. Go on then – tell me what you know".

*"Well, to start with, we cobwebs can be really useful. Cobwebs are the strongest material on earth by weight and we have wonderful healing properties – we are antiseptic and antifungal and rich in vitamin K, which helps blood clotting. The ancient Greeks knew all about us and their soldiers would put vinegar on wounds, pour honey on and then use webs to keep the honey in place. And in **A Midsummer Night's Dream**, one of the characters said 'I shall desire you of more acquaintance, good master cobweb. If I cut my finger, I shall make bold of you' ".*

"How do you know about Shakespeare"?

"I listen to some of your TV programmes. I can't see them from here but I can hear the words".

"Well that's all very interesting, but what does it have to do with business resources".

"Well, I could potentially be a resource for you if you can't find your first aid kit, although I doubt that would please your doctor. But I've been right here under your nose for ages and you haven't noticed me. And I've heard from your TV that it's the same for many businesses".

"What – they have lots of cobwebs"?

"No, many of them have lots of unused resources".

"Oh really, what sort of things are they"?

"They might be ideas that haven't been developed, skills that haven't been applied, existing products that could be used in new ways, money sitting in accounts and not earning interest, government grants that haven't been claimed, books that haven't been read, contacts that haven't been spoken to and even existing employees with skills that haven't been noticed. The list is endless".

"Actually, that's really helpful. OK, you've won your reprieve – you carry on sitting there on the staircase and I'll pass on that information to my business colleagues. But I don't think I'll tell them how I found it, or they'll think I'm spinning them a yarn".

"Just as my spider did – I like it. You've made a cobweb very happy".

Do you have untapped resources in your own business?

BUILDING MUTUALLY BENEFICIAL RELATIONSHIPS

Do you make the most of your business relationships – including in financial terms? There are several ways to grow your business through collaborating with others – as you can find out from this conversation.

SERVING BOWL IN THE CHINA CUPBOARD

"Hello serving bowl. You look a bit sad sitting in the cupboard".

"Well I've not been used for so long and I miss helping your visitors enjoy their food".

"Not much I can do about that at the moment, unfortunately, but I'm sure we'll have more people here before too long. You'll just have to sit it out in the meantime; at least you have the other bowls, and plates and cups and jugs to chat to".

"I know, but my main job is helping people to share things. I sometimes wonder why you humans don't do more of that themselves".

"Well a lot of people do share things of course, like ideas, transport and, of course, food"

"Yes, but business people could do a lot more of it themselves; it could really benefit them".

"How so"?

"Well I can think of three things for starters. See what I did there, I got a food reference in before I began - starters; how smart am I"?

"I'm not going to answer that".

"Anyway, the first thing business people could do is encourage WOMM – word of mouth marketing. Everyone does that naturally – when you read a good book, or find a great shop, you tell your friends about it. And some businesses do that actively by encouraging chat about their products through influencers, social media, product reviews and lots more".

"You said that was the first thing they could do; are there others"?

"Lots, but here are just two more. The first is contra-deals, where businesses trade off products or services without money changing hands (although you might have to record and account for this so you don't get into trouble with the tax people). And the second is affiliate schemes, where you offer incentives to other businesses to promote what you do – for example by giving those businesses a discount voucher on your products or services which they can offer to their own customers so they can add extra value to their own activities".

"That sounds great, serving bowl. I must try some of those things myself. And perhaps I can give you an outing this weekend so you can do some sharing as well; it's the least I can do in return for your advice".

Do you use affiliate schemes or contra-deals already? If not, they're well worth considering.

COPING WITH TECHNOLOGY

Are you IT-savvy or are you (like me) a technophobe?

BOX ON THE TABLE

"Hello sparkly box – I'm trying to remember what's inside you".

"Hello yourself. Fancy forgetting all about me – that's a bit disappointing, especially as I'm a recent addition to a long line of boxes. You know the Egyptians built boxes 3,000 years ago, police signal boxes were introduced in Glasgow in 1891 and the red telephone box started in 1926 after a competition was held to design a kiosk. But clearly that isn't interesting enough for you to come and look at me".

"I didn't say I'd forgotten *YOU*, only what's inside you - it's been a long time since I took off your lid to check".

"Not the only thing you forget! You have the attention span of a gnat".

"That's not true at all; how unkind of you to say so. I can concentrate indefinitely if I choose to".

"Yes, choose is the operative word. I've seen you sitting at your computer typing for hours with no thought at all about what's inside that either".

"Who's interested in what's inside a computer? As long as it works I'm happy".

"That's right, just thinking about yourself again. Don't you want to know how things function".

"No, I don't. People who enjoy it can take care of that".

"Well, at least that's an honest – and sensible - answer. Technology is vital for us all, and it's getting more and more complex as time passes, so it often requires specialist knowledge. If you have a business, then you need to concentrate on the things you do best and buy-in, or trade, services from others for the bits you can't, or don't want to, do".

"I completely agree. I know lots of people who provide business services in areas outside my competence or interest; I need to use more of them in the future so I can spend time on activities I enjoy".

"Glad you've realised that. Now, how about taking my lid off so I can show you all that stuff you've forgotten existed".

What are your personal technology-related achievements or disasters?

STAY ON THE RIGHT SIDE OF THE LAW

Do you know if you're complying with legislation? There's so much of it nowadays that it can be hard to be sure.

KITCHEN KNIVES ON THE TABLE

"Hello knives. You're a great addition to our kitchen".

"Thank you so much – we're very pleased to be of service. Did you know that we Japanese knives have a very long history and the oldest one of us in existence is about 1400 years old. It's a similar shape to a Japanese sword, with a very long handle? Also we traditionally only had bevels on one side, to make fine cutting easier – unlike European knives which are bevelled on both sides"?

"No I didn't know all that. And I'm keeping you in your boxes when you're not in use; you're so sharp it seems a safer thing to do. Also I have a chain mail glove so I can put that on my other hand if I'm doing something that might make you slip – don't want to have an accident".

"That's good to hear. So many people use us for other purposes – knife crime is becoming so prevalent that we're really worried ourselves".

"You're right. Just hope that something can be done about it soon".

"At least most people understand that mis-using knives is a criminal offence. But we guess that a lot of your business associates aren't always aware of when they're breaking the law".

"Do you think that's common"?

"Yes – very often it's done inadvertently. Although, of course, there are lots of deliberate business crimes, such as fraud, bribery, tax evasion, embezzlement, insider trading and money laundering. Mainly though it's likely to be things that business people just lack knowledge about".

"What kind of things are those"?

"All sorts – health and safety infringements, discrimination against particular people, failure to comply with employment law, unauthorised personal use of business property such as cars or computers, insurance regulations, data protection requirements – there's a very long list".

"So anyone going into business really needs to check out those things at the start, to make sure they're doing things legally as well as ethically".

"Exactly. Now what are we going to make today? We're pretty good at cutting up fish, you know, so maybe some nicely shaped pieces of Hake would fit the bill – we saw them come into the kitchen this morning and looked forward to getting our teeth into them".

"My teeth, I think you mean. You haven't any of those as far as I can see".

"Pedantic! But let's get started anyway".

Do you know if you're complying with all the legal requirements for your business? If not, maybe you need to do some research and check it out. Which areas do you find the trickiest to deal with?

SELECTING PEOPLE

Do you have employees? Or associates, or casual staff? If so, how good are your selection processes? Maybe these birds can help..

PARASITE-WOOD BIRDS ON THE WINDOWSILL

"Hello birds, you look as if you're having a meeting".

"Not really – we've just been peeping through the window at the rain – that was quite a downpour last night".

"Certainly was – a drainpipe overflowed and flooded the room below the flat roof – could have done without that".

"Actually it reminded us of Bali, where we came from. The monsoons there are quite something – they make your little rainstorms look insignificant".

"I didn't know you were from Bali; that's interesting".

"Yes, we come from Chinaberry trees. We're parasites, a bit like mushrooms, which feed on the sap of the trees. We get so hard that, when our host tree dies and rots away, we remain and can be carved into flowers or animals or whatever the wood carver chooses. And sometimes the carvings are done from the tree itself, where one of us has been attached and the tree's formed a shape round it. It's quite a tradition".

"So what were you talking about before I arrived".

"We were discussing what we'd look for if a new bird joined us. We think we'd go for one who could tell us interesting stories, because it can get quite boring hearing our own tales over and over again. Of course, if we were running a business, like some of your colleagues, we'd be more discriminating".

"Glad to hear that. So what exactly would you look for if you were taking on new people in a business".

"Well, given that we're not human, we don't have any expertise in recruitment, but we think a good starting point would be their personality and how it might fit with colleagues or customers; how well they could communicate with – and work with - other people; and then relevant knowledge, experience and skills - or the willingness and motivation to develop them. Oh, and a sense of humour for when things go wrong – as they sometimes do".

"That's a great list birds. Anything else"?

"Only that people selecting others should have the skills needed to make those assessments. So often you humans seem to come to conclusions on hardly any evidence, so it's important to be able to ask good questions, observe how someone answers and give them the opportunity to really demonstrate what they're like and how good a fit they'd be".

"Good advice. Now tell me what kind of bird you'd like me to look out for to join your little group".

"Thought we'd done that already – one who would fit in, tell us funny stories and be good at sitting on a shelf – that pretty much sums it up. Now please go and find one".

What would YOU look for in an employee or colleague?

WELCOMING DIVERSITY

Do you work on your own, or with other people? Either way, how much diversity is there in your life and your business? Do you have diverse interests, diverse activities, diversity in your colleagues or customers or friends? And is your business really inclusive? May be worth evaluating.

PUMPKINS IN THE WASHROOM

"Hello pumpkins. Great to have you here".

"Good to see you too. It's a change from the pumpkin farm where we were raised, but it seems a nice place to be".

"Hope so. It was difficult knowing which of you to pick; there were literally thousands of pumpkins in those fields".

"We were used to it of course – all of us side by side as we grew".

"And you're all so different; different sizes, different colours, different shapes and (dare I mention it) no doubt different tastes once you're cooked".

"It's OK. We know what we're here for and it makes us feel valued and useful. It's OK to be eaten as long as it's done respectfully. It would be good if you humans were as happy as we are with diversity".

"Well of course we're all different too".

"Yes, but not everyone realises that. From what we've heard, some businesses aren't very good at accepting and catering for diversity. We pumpkins vary in size, shape and colour, which humans do too, but you have lots more differences, like behaviour, attitudes, beliefs, thought processes, physical capabilities and much more. It's only fair to do what you can to accommodate differences between individuals".

"Very true. People can be capable and productive whatever their personal circumstances".

"By the way, did you know we pumpkins have an interesting past? We originated in America over 7,000 years ago and, strictly speaking, we're fruits – not vegetables. And our name's changed a lot – first it was Pepon (in Greek), then Pompon (in French), then Pumpion (in English) – and Shakespeare referred to Pumpions in one of his plays. Then American colonists changed Pumpion into Pumpkin".

"That's quite a history".

"Yes, and we haven't only been used for food, although in the 17th century creating pumpkin recipes was something women could do to reach an audience. Native Americans dried us and wove us into mats and the largest pumpkin weighed over 2,000lbs. Oh, and humans in Ireland made us into lanterns because of a myth about someone making an agreement with the devil – Jack O'Lanterns we were called. Then they took that tradition with them to the United States.

"How do you know all that, pumpkins"?

"Our parents told us those stories when we were just seeds, and we remembered, so now we can tell you".

"How lovely. And when I cook you I must take account of your own diversity and come up with something different for each of you. It's the least I can do".

"Certainly is"!

How do you approach diversity in your business?

TEAM ROLES

Are you part of a team, or are you a freelancer? Different roles are needed in business and they can apply either to teams or individuals. See if these little objects can throw some light on what's required.

SEWING KIT IN THE DRESSING ROOM

"Hello sewing things. I need you today".

"Well, there's a rare occurrence; it's not often you call on us, given your lack of sewing skills".

"I can only agree, but just occasionally I have to do some repairs for myself. Although it's not my favourite occupation (no offence intended of course)".

"None taken. What would you like us to do for you"?

"I have a cardigan with horrible buttons and sleeves that are too long. If we're all going to help the environment and keep our carbon footprint down, then we need to buy fewer new clothes and make do with the ones we have already".

"I know all about that".

"Who said that"?

"It's me – the oldest reel of cotton. I was around during the war and everyone was talking about make-do and mend, so I'm pleased it's coming back again".

"OK, so where do we start"?

"We think you should take a leaf out of your business books and consider team roles".

"And how do you know about those"?

"When you leave our drawer open we can see some of your books. It seems that effective human teams divide up activities to make best use of individuals' talents. So how about doing that with your cardigan alteration. Can you remember what the different team roles are? As a hint, several were identified by someone called Meredith Belbin".

"I think Belbin said one team role is driving the team forward, one is co-ordinating the team, one is coming up with ideas, one is planning a strategy, one is investigating useful resources, one is undertaking specialist activities, one is monitoring things in a logical way, one is ensuring that details are dealt with and one is helping the team to gel".

"Yes, and even if someone is working on their own, and not as part of a team, they're still likely to need all those elements, but if they don't have them personally they can buy some in or trade some off. So, for this task, can we suggest that you come up with the ideas and co-ordinate us all as a team, the tape measure plans the strategy for shortening the sleeves, the buttons agree amongst themselves which are needed as resources, the needles push things forward (they should be great at that), the stitch unpicker gives specialist help in taking off the old buttons, the magnifying specs help you see the details, the chalk marker monitors progress and the reels of cotton help everyone to work together harmoniously".

"That sounds excellent; I can see exactly how it will work now".

"You mean you can see exactly how ***we*** *will work now; not sure about your input though".*

"Cheek. But thanks for your help".

Which are your strongest or weakest team roles?

ACCESSIBILITY

Do you consider how easy it is for people to find your business? Are your premises and your website easily accessible for everyone? Do you take care to cater for those who want your services? Maybe there's some useful information from this little pig.

NURSING SOW ON THE RADIATOR

"Hello sow. You aren't looking your most cheerful today".

"Neither would you be if you had to feed ten hungry piglets".

"I expect not. Feeding ten hungry people at a dinner party is more than enough for me – and that's just a one-off, not several times a day".

"And that's why I'm getting a bit thin now – it's time for the babies to start fending for themselves rather than relying on me all the time. Although I have to say they are rather good at getting their milk. Did you know that each piglet has its own teat and always comes to the same place at the milk bar for each meal"?

"Yes, I did know that. I've seen real piglets squabbling as soon as they're born and the strongest ones getting the teats at the front, which give them a better supply of milk and helps them grow even faster than the smaller piglets".

"It's all about accessibility really. The front teats of pigs are spaced more widely than the ones further back, and this makes it easier for their piglets to get to them when their mums lie down. It would be good if some of your business colleagues considered accessibility too, you know".

"I beg your pardon. My colleagues don't go around offering their bosoms to people – that would be quite unacceptable".

"No, you've misunderstood me. I meant they should consider how accessible their businesses are to visitors. Can a wheelchair user get into their premises? Can people with poor vision, or dyslexia, use their website easily? Do they have a statement on their website offering help to people who need it? Do they – for example – say 'Follow this link' rather than 'Click here', because 'here' may not be clear to the person wanting the information".

"Gosh, that's a lot to think about, sow. Do you think it really matters if they do all that"?

"Only if they want to attract more customers, help people with a disability and stay on the right side of equal opportunities law. Otherwise it doesn't matter at all".

"Well I shall have to make sure they get this information – and you'll have to make sure your piglets get weaned soon – then everyone can be pleased with a job well done".

Do you have an accessibility statement on your website?

BUILD YOUR SUCCESS ONLINE

Is what you offer available online?

CLOTHES PEGS ON THE DESK

"Hello clothes pegs – welcome to our house".

"Thank you; we're excited to be here".

"I was talking to some other business owners and they said they were doing really well on line, so I thought I'd better buy you".

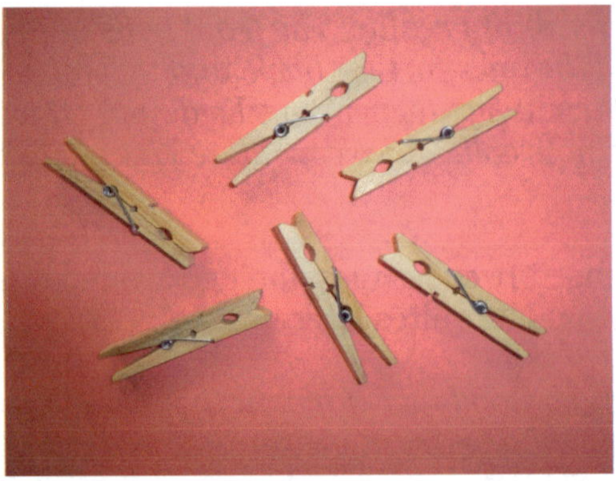

"Really, what's the connection".

"They said they were doing well ON LINE, so I knew I needed clothes pegs".

"How silly are you? They didn't mean on line; they meant online".

"Well how's that different"?

"On line is what we do – we hold your clothes on a line to dry".

"I know that – it's why I bought you".

"Gordon Bennett. Online is about using devices like computers and phones and laptops – and even watches – to use the internet. And if you have a business it's essential to do that".

"So I didn't need to buy you then – I wasted my money".

"Clearly you didn't. If nobody else has told you these things, buying us was a very small investment for the information".

"OK, clever clogs. If you know so much, what should I be doing on the internet"?

"You should have a website, get on social media, do some videos, publish some articles or blogs, have an online shop if you sell stuff (by the way 'stuff' is a technical term for products and services),consider doing podcasts and take time to investigate resources such as information, research, courses and so on. Can't get anywhere nowadays without all that".

"How come you know about technology"?

"Clothes pegs are very smart. Or at least....we could have been. Peg-like objects were found in Egyptian tombs, although we weren't used for hanging clothes until the 19th century. However, an Australian laundry brand called OMO, started trials of a smartpeg, called Peggy, which could send messages from your washing line to your smartphone telling you when your sheets were dry, and when it was going to rain. It checked UV light, humidity and temperature and combined this information with scientific formulas about the rate at which clothes dry. Apparently if you know what light is actually hitting your washing, and how much humidity there is in the air, you can tell pretty accurately when it will be dry. Although we don't think Peggy is actually available, word spreads quickly in the clothes peg community, so we all know about the internet and how it can be used effectively".

"Well, well – we live and learn. Or at least humans do – pegs, on the other hand, just hang out on lines".

What could you do to improve your online presence?

PLANNING FOR, AND SAFEGUARDING, THE FUTURE

Do you have plans in place in case of adversity? May be worth considering.....

CUSHIONS ON THE COUCH

"Hello cushions. Are you enjoying yourselves in here"?

"Sort of. It's been very quiet, of course, with no visitors, but we do have the other cushions to chat to if we're bored".

"You're a bit different from them though. They're used all the time, whereas you're more for occasional use if the need arises".

"Bit like what happens in business then. Business people need cushions for emergencies".

"I thought they needed desks and chairs – although I must admit I did have a small cushion on my old typing chair to make it less hard".

"No, we don't mean business people need cushions to sit on; we mean they need cushions in case of difficult times".

"What cushions might those be"?

"Some money in the bank in case income dries up for a while; someone to take over if they're ill, a succession plan for longer term development, enough stock or components to tide them over if orders increase rapidly, and maybe back-up computer systems in case something crashes".

"I've never thought of those things as cushions, but you've put a different perspective on it. After all, cushions do make you more comfortable".

"We certainly do. Did you know that we've been around for about nine thousand years – starting in ancient Mesopotamia. In the Middle Ages cushions were used to sit on, usually by lower ranking people in a household. And the more cushions you owned, the more affluent you were seen to be. And, of course, hard 'cushions' were used to support the heads of mummies in ancient Egyptian tombs".

"Well, I'd never have thought of those as cushions – at least our modern ones, like you, are much softer. And thanks for letting me know about cushions for business".

"You're very welcome - now make sure you spread the word".

What cushions does your own business have?

PROTECTION IN CASE OF DISASTER

Do you have systems in place to protect your business? Maybe you could learn something from this little object.

PARASOL AT THE SIDE OF THE CUPBOARD

"Hello parasol. Not been much call for you this summer".

"No. I've been a bit depressed here in the corner, with just a couple of umbrellas to keep me company".

"Well I didn't like to keep you on your own completely. I hope the umbrellas have been reasonably sociable".

"Yes, we've chatted quite a lot over the months. The umbrellas were actually pretty glad they weren't needed – can't say I felt the same. But then I felt really proud to be a parasol; I'm important - just like certain things in business".

"What do you mean, parasol"?

"Well – like the umbrellas – I protect you when needed. And that's the kind of thing that business owners do – have something to protect them but hope it's not needed".

"Why on earth is that required; surely we don't have protection rackets here".

"No, that's not what I meant. I mean protection in case of business disaster. That could be insurance in case of fire or floods or business interruption, or for professional liability or serious illness or injury, or theft. Then there's password protection to stop hackers and IT back-up in case of systems failure. And there's protection for intellectual property rights – and more".

"I see. And you said you felt proud – what do you feel proud about in particular?

"I'm proud that parasols like me have been used by humans for thousands of years. Did you know we're much older than umbrellas and we developed into ones you'd recognise about four thousand years ago in ancient Egypt, Assyria and China. We used to be made from trees and branches, and then animal skins, cloth and paper. Because we cost so much, we were mainly used by important people such as royalty and the clergy and we protected them from the hot sun. So I know that, if the need arises, I'm more than happy to come out from the corner and look after you".

"Good to know – and I'll spread the word about business protection and also encourage my friends to keep at last one parasol in preparation for global warming".

Does your business have protection in place?

JOIN A PROFESSIONAL BODY

Are you a member of a professional body? If not, maybe this will influence you.

COMFORTABLE CHAIR IN THE CONSERVATORY

"Hello chair. You're one of my favourites".

"Glad to hear it; it's good to be appreciated. Did you know that wicker furniture like me (well, perhaps not exactly like me) has been around almost 5,000 years, since the ancient Egyptians wove rattan. And the word 'wicker' is of Scandinavian origin and comes from Wika, which means to bend, and Vikker, which means willow".

“How interesting. So are you like some of those early chairs then”?

“No, I think I’m more like one of those professional bodies you talk about from time to time”.

“How on earth do you think you’re like one of those?

“Well, I’m here to support you”.

“Errrr. I think they do more than that, you know”.

“Really, what sort of things”?

“Well they let you meet other people with similar interests and activities”.

“I do that too. When you have visitors, they sit in the other chairs here so you can chat and exchange ideas”.

“Hmmmm. Not sure that’s quite the same really”.

“And I also help you learn new things and develop your skills, just like those organisations do”.

“No you don’t”.

“Yes, I do. If you weren’t comfortable, you’d never be able to give your full attention to all those books you read”.

“Well you don’t give me a certificate of achievement or attendance at events”.

"So you don't think the marks on your bum show that you've been sitting here too long then. Don't you feel that's a kind of attendance certificate"?

"No, I don't. And I don't sit here for hours on end anyway, so that's a bit of a specious argument".

"Don't you go using your long words with me. I'm not easily impressed".

"No, you're embossed, not impressed. I know that. So let's sum up. You don't run courses or issue certificates showing my status in a profession, you don't provide meetings or conferences where I can meet other similar people, you don't help me promote my business, you don't represent me in disputes, you don't give me insurance cover for my work, you don't have an advice line, you don't publish a list of members, you don't get media coverage for my type of business and you don't have a logo I can use online or on my printed material. So how exactly are you like a professional body"?

"You know I'm always there if you need me. Isn't that what professional bodies are about really"?

Is being a member of a professional body important to you?

NOTICING YOUR GROWTH

At some stage, businesses can outgrow a single person. It's important to notice if you're reaching this stage.

FROG IN THE CORNER

"Hello frog. It's almost time for you to go out into the garden again. You're better off indoors here in the winter, so the frost doesn't get to you, but you come into your element outside when it's warmer".

"Yes, I'm looking forward to that too. Nice to have the sunshine on me and see all the birds and other animals that pass by. I believe you have lots of real frogs outside as well".

"Yes, and in our cellar too – although how they get in is anyone's guess".

"Well it must be nice seeing them develop – I came ready made, so to speak, but they go through lots of stages in their lives".

"They do – they start off as eggs, then hatch into tiny tadpoles, then they start making the most of the pond and swimming around all over the place. And then they develop into small froglets and, if they're lucky, become proper frogs like you".

"A bit like some businesses, of course. They start out tiny, just one person, and then some of them grow into huge organisations. But not all of them seem to recognise they've outgrown their circumstances and pretend they can stay as tadpoles when, in reality, they need to turn into a frog".

"That's a nice way of putting it. Recognise when your business has outgrown your abilities to do everything, or to grow, and add resources – including new people – when that stage has come about".

"Quite. Now, if we've finished the lesson for today, can you take me over to the door to see out. Even if it's not yet time to leave the security of this warm room, I'd like a glimpse of what the future is going to bring".

How will you recognise when it's not appropriate to stay as a sole trader, doing everything yourself?

WHAT'S IN IT FOR THEM?
Community and beyond

No business exists in isolation – we are all part of a wider community. Being successful and making a profit is essential, but it's also important to make a difference, and to give back, to others.

Community engagement and social enterprise are all about working collaboratively with others and helping those who are less fortunate. It's about being part of, and supporting, both your local community and further afield.

And considering environmental issues is vital, because global warming and scarcity of resources affects us all.

Here are just a few ideas on these topics:

USE LOCAL RESOURCES

Tapping into local suppliers can benefit both you and them.

BAY LEAVES ON THE COUNTER

"Hello bay leaves. I need some of you today. Glad you're always there in your jar".

"We enjoy being in the kitchen and watching what goes on; especially when things go wobbly – we like a good laugh"

"How unkind. Things don't go wobbly often – trust you to notice the odd occasion when they do".

"Well we can see everything through the glass sides of our jar and it's more fun when something silly happens – a good break from everyday activities. Not that bay is an everyday leaf, of course".

"No, I certainly don't use you every day".

"That's not what we meant. We were talking about our history. People used to associate bay leaves with goodness, and saw us as a protection against evil. Roman generals were crowned with bay leaves after victorious battles and Greek athletes were given wreaths of bay – often referred to as laurels - when they were victorious and so were emperors, poets and writers. And the terms baccalaureate and bachelor for academic degrees are derived from baccalaures (laurel berry), because of the ancient Greek and Roman practice of honouring scholars and poets with garlands of bay branches. Roman soldiers added the leaves to their baths to soothe fatigue and injuries and some people nowadays put bay leaves on their fires, so the oil in them rises in the air and helps them feel calm and relaxed".

"That's an impressive background – you've certainly been well used through the ages. And now you're pretty common in kitchens".

"Yes, but not everyone has a bay tree in their garden like you do".

"No, that's one of the first things we've always done when we've moved to a new house – plant a bay tree. Although our last house had one in the garden already; huge it was, over thirty feet high".

"Well it's sensible to plant one - have you seen the prices of bay leaves in the shops nowadays – extortionate! But also, by having a tree in your garden you've adopted a good business practice too".

"Oh, a know-it-all bunch of bay leaves! What's that then"?

"Using local resources. It's great to hire local craftspeople or technicians, go to a local enterprise centre or even use a local person to baby-sit for you while you're working. Good for the environment as it involves less travel and wonderful to support local traders.

So having a local bay tree – and you can't get much more local than your own garden - is excellent. Well done you"!

What local resources do you use in your business?

CONSIDER ENVIRONMENTAL ISSUES

Does your business waste resources? Do you think about environmental issues on a day-to-day basis? Do you know how best to make use of existing materials? Perhaps this conversation will help.

PLASTIC-BAG HENS ON THE FLOOR

"Hello hens – you look chirpy today".

"Yes, we would chirp if we could. We enjoy the sunshine – it cheers us up and shows off our shiny feathers. But it's just as well we don't need feeding as there isn't any corn on this carpet".

"No, you've been pretty maintenance-free since you arrived a long time ago. Just an occasional dust and that's about it".

"An occasional dust – we don't remember being dusted ***at all****. Are you sure you've got your facts right"?*

"I thought I had, but perhaps I've forgotten. Anyway, you look pretty good to me".

"Well that's because we're made of plastic, which lasts for ever. Well, maybe not absolutely for ever, but for a very long time. Did you know it's been calculated that bottles and disposable nappies can take 450 years to decompose. Plastic straws can take 200 years and disposable plastic cups can take 50 years. Even plastic bags like the ones we're made of can take 20 years to break down".

"I thought plastic didn't decompose at all".

"Well now you're being nit-picky. Most plastics don't decompose like organic material, because organisms such as bacteria don't generally work on them. But a lot of plastic breaks down into smaller and smaller pieces until it ends up as micro-plastics and a lot of that gets into rivers and oceans and then into creatures who live there, or who drink that water".

"But people use so much plastic that it's hard to imagine them stopping and finding alternatives".

"We know. Look at what goes on in most businesses - printers that are cheaper to throw away than buy new ink for, packaging that's unnecessary and wasteful, new phones being bought when they're not needed – and lots more. That's why the three Rs are so important – recycle, re-use and reduce. And all three apply to us hens".

"How's that"?

*"We're **recycled** from plastic bags; you've given us a **new use** – as ornaments – and we've **reduced** your spending on newly-made items which might use more energy and materials than we took in being made".*

"That sounds great. And of course there are more Rs, like repair, or refurbish or restore or even regurgitate".

"That's disgusting. Nobody's going to make something out of stuff that's been sicked-up".

"Well my dogs used to eat their sick, so maybe having your meal twice is a good way of saving on food bills. Must give it a try".

"Gordon Bennett! We thought we were odd, but that takes the biscuit (twice)"!

How does your business avoid waste or make better use of resources?

BE INVOLVED WITH SOCIAL ENTERPRISE AND LOCAL COMMUNITIES

Do you give back to your community?

TEACUP IN THE KITCHEN

"Hello teacup. You're really big – one almost needs to be a weight-lifter to pick you up when you're full".

"Well a lot of people really like their tea. Did you know that tea drinking started in China over 2,000 years ago and was then taken to Japan by Buddhist monks who had been studying in China? It was first introduced to the UK in the middle of the fifteenth century, when the 'China Drink' went on sale in a coffee house. It wasn't too popular at first, but then it started being offered at temperance meetings as a substitute for alcohol, to persuade 'the working classes' to go teetotal and it really took off after that".

"I didn't know all that, but many years ago some Japanese visitors held a little tea ceremony for us when we lived in London. It was a bit odd to be standing in the middle of our kitchen, in a circle, bowing to each other and handing round a small bowl of green tea, but it was an interesting event".

"Yes, that does sound a little strange. But what about me? It's sad I don't get an outing more often, but I know I'm appreciated when I do see visitors".

"You were quite a find, actually. You're a lovely fine china, despite being so large, and your pattern cheers everyone up".

"I know. Modern cups can be quite boring, can't they – like some of the plain white ones I share the cupboard with. Minimalism is all very well, but colour and patterns brighten up people's days".

"I absolutely agree. And while we're on the subject of brightening things up – is there anything I can do to make your days better"?

"It would be wonderful to have more visitors. And if some of them could be local people who need some support, that would be great. And it makes good business sense too, you know"?

"How does having tea help anyone's business? I don't think I follow you".

"Perhaps you haven't heard of social enterprise then; it's all about helping people and communities – especially those with particular social needs. Of course it's a great thing to do anyway, but a good business reputation is vital for success, and helping others is an important element nowadays for businesses which want to be seen to support those in need. And, of course, supporting other local businesses is great too – not because they have social needs, but because it makes sense in lots of ways to help them out by using their services".

"Yes, I understand, but I'm still not sure how having tea fits into social enterprise".

"Oh dear – I'll have to spell it out, won't I? You may not have lots of spare money in your business to give away to good causes, but you could perhaps invite some people who are feeling lonely, or who can't afford cakes or biscuits with their tea, to join you from time to time. They would benefit from interacting with others and it's a simple way of giving something back to your community".

"I see. Yes, that sounds a good idea – happy to give it a try".

"And when you make your millions, you can give lots of money to people or organisations where it can make a difference – that's what it's all about".

How can you give back to your community?

WHAT NEXT

If you've found this book useful, please do explore what else is out there for you.

- There are organisations for business people – such as FSB (The Federation of Small Businesses), which offer help, support, information, advice, training, networking opportunities and much more.

- There are organisations for specific business functions, such as HR, finance, manufacturing, marketing, export etc.

- There are organisations for specific types of business, such as food, furniture, technology, clothing and much more.

- And there are books, videos, podcasts and courses on all these topics and areas.

- There are also sources of funding and investment, which can be important to businesses at various stages of their development.

- And there are growing numbers of business coaches and mentors for you to work with.

Do check the credentials of people and organisations you are considering learning from or being associated with – and then the world's your oyster (and if I'd had one of those I'd probably have chatted to it in this book).

INTERESTED IN MORE?

If you enjoyed this book there are two more in the same series:

- **Chats with Comestibles** – is all about personal effectiveness
- **Words Speak for Themselves** – is all about writing and language

ACKNOWLEDGMENTS

Thanks to my husband Paul for reading the manuscript, making suggestions and doing the production work on the book. And also to my sister Val Erde for helping with graphics.

And thanks to everyone who read the book pre-publication and made comments or wrote reviews and testimonials.

ABOUT THE AUTHOR

Carol Harris has been helping people improve their personal and business skills for over 30 years. She uses NLP (Neuro-Linguistic Programming) techniques as the foundation for much of her work.

Carol was Chair of the Association for Neuro-Linguistic Programming for some years. She is a Fellow of the Chartered Institute of Personnel and development and was a Fellow and Council Member of the Chartered Institute of Management Consultants. Her last employed role was as one of the Directors of the Arts Council of Great Britain and she has run various businesses of her own including publishing a magazine for management consultants, doing corporate training and having a thriving international network marketing business.

She lives in mid-Wales with her husband, Paul.

OTHER BOOKS BY CAROL HARRIS

For adults

Chats with Comestibles
Words Speak for Themselves
NLP Made Easy
Networking for Success
Think Yourself Slim
Consult Yourself
A Guide to Traditional Pig Keeping
Producing Successful Magazines, Newsletters and E-zines
Some Stories of my Life
The Earning Curve
The Trainer's Cookbook
Co-author: Breakthrough Language Learning

For children

Adventures of the Chickalloon
Adventures of the Hogball
Adventures of the Meerflat

OTHER BOOKS IN THIS SERIES

These books will help you grow your confidence, build good relationships, improve your communications and develop lots of skills so that you'll be more effective in your personal life and in business.

Written in the same style, they are companions to
Lessons from the Speechless.

CHATS WITH COMESTIBLES
Life lessons from food – how to be resourceful, resilient and get results

Would you like to be better at:

- Managing your thoughts, feelings, behaviour
- Building good relationships with others
- Achieving success in your chosen activities

Listen in on conversations with very opinionated food ingredients. Learn simple things you can do to become more effective. Add to your knowledge and skills..... and cook better

This book will entertain you while you improve your performance.

WORDS SPEAK FOR THEMSELVES
How to improve your writing

Would you like to:

- Understand the power of words
- Improve your written communications
- Achieve your writing goals

Listen in on humorous conversations with very opinionated punctuation marks, emojis, metaphors and more. Learn simple ways of becoming a more effective communicator. Add to your knowledge and skills.

This book will get you going or enhance your existing skills

Made in United States
Troutdale, OR
11/03/2026

56852521R00071